THE PURPOSE-DRIVEN SCHOOL

Nadia,
Good luck on your
Journey as a
Purpose Driven
educator !!

S. B

4/2023

EVERY SCHOOL DEFINES THE *FUTURE*

THE
PURPOSE
DRIVEN
SCHOOL

SHAWN BROWN-BRUMFIELD

CREATIVITY, PERSPECTIVE, EXPANSION

DEAN & LEIGH
—— PUBLISHING LLC ——

Printed in the United States of America
Cover Design by Jasmin Williams

Requests for information should be addressed to:

Dean & Leigh Publishing, LLC
1443 E. Washington Blvd. #235
Pasadena, CA 91104
Dean.leighpublishing@gmail.com
www.thepurposedrivenschool.com

LCCN: 2021917043
ISBN: 978-1-7377058-0-2
ISBN (hardcover): 978-1-7377058-1-9

To my wonderful kids, Joseph and Sydney.
Thank you so much for allowing me to pursue my purpose.
You have been true blessings in my life. Thank you
so much for your input and support on this book.
I love you both to the moon and back.

To my family, who has had unwavering support
for me along my journey.

To my true friends, I know that we did not meet by chance.
It was part of God's divine plan. Our kindred spirits were destined
to be together. Thank you so much for your love and support.
I couldn't do what I do without you.

To the Rosebud family, who have been a part
of this amazing journey and experience. Thank you
so much for your dedication and support.

Last but not least . . .

I dedicate this book to all the educators around
the world who are committed to improving humanity and the
world through their impact on children, teens, and young adults.
You are the true heroes in this world,
and your work is invaluable.

TABLE OF CONTENTS

Those who live a life of service find their greatness. Those who live a life of love through education find their humanity.

—SHAWN BROWN-BRUMFIELD

The Calling: Passion into Purpose

"Once you decide to follow your life purpose,
you will only need to pack one thing: your heart!"
—ROXANA JONES, *life coach and author*

When I tell people that I received my bachelor's degree in economics, they find it a bit odd because I have spent my career in the field of education. I entered the educational arena more than two decades ago, shortly after completing my undergraduate studies. Becoming an educator was never on my radar when I was growing up or while in college. So, I can only explain arriving here as destiny.

I started my career in education as a substitute teacher at a middle school in the town where I grew up. It did not take long for me to be hired as a full-time teacher with my own classes. After a few years of teaching, I became passionate about education, which compelled me to obtain my teaching credential and a master's degree in educational leadership. By the time I completed my master's, I had become so fascinated and obsessed with the educational process, I knew I had found my life's purpose.

When passion meets destiny, that dynamic becomes an art. Education became an art for me. Unconsciously, I spent days and nights trying to figure out how to make what is complicated about education simple. I was constantly questioning how we can improve learning for *all students*. That drive and determination led me to open a charter school. From there, I began to take an even closer look at the details of creating the optimal educational environment conducive to student learning.

Obedient to the Calling

Attending college opened my eyes to the education that I had received in grades K-12. I discovered that there were gaps in my academic proficiencies. I lacked what appeared to be common knowledge and certain foundational academic skills. In order to survive the rigors of college, I used my intellect to make up for these deficiencies. Eventually, I was able to find a balance between the two to obtain a bachelor's and then a master's degree. Looking back, I wholeheartedly believe that my personal educational journey played a role in my commitment and dedication to education. It set the tone for my calling and what has become my life's work.

When I became a middle school teacher, I was determined to set students up for long-term success. I started connecting the dots from my experience in elementary school, middle school, high school, and college. I knew the thread that connected a child's compulsory education had to be strong to prepare them for the demands of college and later, a career. Initially, my approach in the classroom was dictated by my academic career. It played a huge role in how I interpreted teaching and learning. College allowed me to understand the importance of educational sequencing as it relates to the long-term curricular and instructional planning for academic success. As I became more seasoned in my teaching practice, I refined what I understood about my primary and secondary learning experiences and applied it to the culture of education at that time. My organizational skills, coupled with my youthful personality, allowed me to connect with the students and create great classroom dynamics. The combination of curricular and instructional backwards mapping, state standards, and effective classroom structure was a major component to implementing grade-level curriculum for college and career readiness. I realized that in order to successfully prepare students for long-term academic success, they needed both a strong academic and social foundation in elementary school. Without it, students would struggle in middle school, high school, and beyond.

As a teacher, my perception and perspective on education was limited. It wasn't until I founded Pasadena Rosebud Academy Charter School in September 2007 that I gained both a broad and detailed knowledge and experience of the social, structural, academic, and financial implementation of school business. There is a wide scope and a narrow focus that plays a role in education. As the founder of a charter school, I was challenged to create a vision for educating students and to develop a holistic, detailed plan that could be implemented. In order to do that I had to get in tune with my instincts, as well as my own educational and life experiences, to navigate the processes it would take to create the ideal learning, working, and familial environment for all stakeholders.

In my role as founder and director of a charter school, I learned the administrative, curricular, instructional, and financial responsibilities that are associated with the day-to-day operations of a school. My senses were heightened to every aspect of educational business and the intricacies of education as a whole. This position allowed me to understand the full dynamics of education and how all components translate to student achievement. My life and educational experiences have prepared me for this calling: to impact the lives of the students I encounter and use my educational insight to improve the quality of schools around the globe. My experience as a teacher, founder, and administrator at Pasadena Rosebud Academy inspired me to write *The Purpose-Driven School*.

Creating Vitality in Schools

*"The future of humanity and our world
is at the mercy of schools. The education of our youth
defines the continued success of our country."*

—SHAWN BROWN-BRUMFIELD,
educator and author

Education is critical to creating and preserving the ecosystem of humanity. As the world grows smaller due to technological advancements, it will be the language of humanity that allows us to connect in a harmonious way as a human race. Education is a vehicle to achieving global awareness and unity.

In a changing world, education must support the advancement of mankind, racial accord, technology, and effective communication. Schools are charged with the task of educating students in a way that will create global harmony and economic growth. The role that education plays in our world is so vast and vital to the progress of all things that enhance our planet socially and economically. Now more than ever, we as a country must take a serious look at education as we know it today. The world keeps turning, but education seems to be standing still.

The state of education continues to tell the same story, and that narrative has to change. To ensure that the world is continuously fueled year after year, decade after decade, and century after century, schools must have tools to create and maintain *vitality*. According to Dictionary.com, vitality is the "capacity for survival or for the continuation of a meaningful or purposeful existence." It is further described as the "power to live, grow, or develop." Schools are essential to the advancement of humanity and our world; as such, it is imperative that educational leaders have the ability to create continuity of meaningful and purposeful existence for the long haul. In order to do so, schools should be considered forms of life that need sustenance to grow and thrive. Vitality in schools is equivalent to the heartbeat and breath of the human body. The decisions that educational leaders make are the heart and lungs of education, and the impact of those decisions will determine the strength of the heartbeat and breath, or its vitality. Ultimately, long-term vitality in schools will be determined by the actions that educational administrative leaders take and the outcome of their decisions. Vitality can and will be created when there is an intentional effort to support the immediate and future success of schools, which is predicated on the high academic performance and accomplishments of *all students*.

Vitality in schools, like other businesses, requires leaders to be progressive thinkers with an eye on longevity. Far too often, educators are myopic in their vision and planning. The idea of vitality in schools involves not only sustainability and progress—it involves thriving long-term. Vitality should be part of the conversation when planning and setting goals, and that means taking a close look at how school business and management decisions, at all levels, impact student learning over 3-10 years. Forecasting and ongoing evaluation of policies and procedures in all areas of school business and operations have to include long-term projections in curriculum planning, instructional design, human resources, fiscal impact, and facilities, among many others.

To survive and thrive every successive decade, schools must predict future educational trends and models based on social, political, economic, and technological developments. Factors that schools need to consider when building the capacity to thrive are long-term strategic planning, technological advancements, adaptability, political climate, and quality vs. quantity.

Long-Term Strategic Planning

Future planning is the bedrock of vitality in schools. Long-term strategic planning puts educational leaders in the driver's seat of school success. As school leaders construct a vision of vitality, a 3–5-year strategic plan needs to be created that outlines and measures where the school is in terms of meeting their overall mission and vision, as well as determines what needs to occur moving forward to achieve the school's goals. The strategic plan provides a built-in structure that calls for consistent assessment and reevaluation of practices to ensure that they are meeting the ultimate goal of student achievement. By anticipating how time will influence education and business practices, administrators and leaders can better acclimate to educational conditions and advancements in the future.

The advancement of technology is integral to every school's strategic planning.

Technological Advancements

The Information Age was born from the advancement of technology, which makes technology synonymous with education. It is the most viable channel for accessing existing information, and it continually generates new knowledge. Embracing the information/digital age is the first step in producing vitality in schools. As information becomes readily available with new technology, it is imperative that students are provided with access, resources, knowledge, skills, and connectivity to keep pace with technological improvements and remain academically and socially relevant.

The expansion of technology has a direct effect on the future success of students. College and career preparedness relies heavily on technology. When students graduate from high school, they need to possess advanced technology skills, competencies, and confidence to be competitive in college and ultimately find success in the workforce. For students to develop technological expertise, teachers have to maintain an advanced level of technology skills themselves and incorporate technology into their regular instructional practices.

Ongoing professional development centered around technology is necessary to support student growth and the implementation of practices that support technology instruction and learning. Being aware of current and future technological advancements is fundamental to providing students with a quality education.

In addition to the classroom, business operations must also maintain technological infrastructures that improve efficiency in record-keeping, internal and external communication, productivity, and overall quality of service. The enhanced efficiency and systems that these innovations can deliver are essential to maintaining school vitality. Having the ability to adapt to ever-changing technology is imperative to a school's progress.

Adaptability

The ability to adapt is also important to the goal of creating vitality in schools. The future of education is determined by many factors that are sometimes unpredictable. Being able to adapt to unforeseen changes or situations allows schools to adjust their sails to the changing winds and currents of educational circumstances. This allows schools to avoid disruption to the mission and vision of the school. The 2020 COVID-19 pandemic was a telltale sign of how essential adaptation is to surviving and thriving in the educational world. Schools that were able to transition to distance learning with relative ease were able to maximize teaching and learning.

Recognizing change is a natural part of life. Educators need to process and embrace the importance of adaptability. The inability to adapt to changing circumstances will lead schools into stagnation and will have serious consequences on the school and student performance. All staff members have to be willing to engage with the vicissitudes of change that affect education because the success of each school is ultimately a group effort. The resilience of the staff will determine the school's capacity to adapt expeditiously to technological advancements, social and economic impact, and political changes.

Political Climate

Political leaders have a huge influence on education. They are constantly creating bills and laws that have a direct impact on our schools. Politicians make decisions based on experiences, beliefs, assumptions, and trends. Special interest groups often influence political decisions by pressuring politicians to support what they consider important for students and schools. With different agendas in play, educators need to keep a finger on the pulse of the political climate. This makes it possible to navigate the implementation of educational policies and adjust to any modifications at the school site in a way that minimizes any potential damage to the progress of student achievement. As political leaders enter and exit office, a revolving door of policies will negatively or positively affect education. Amid the uncertainty and changing political mood, leaders in education can support their staff by being ready to implement new policies efficiently so staff can remain focused on maintaining the quality of ongoing educational practices.

Quality vs. Quantity

Being better is always the goal. Oftentimes educational leaders buy into the misnomer that more is better. But the goal should always be to focus on quality, not quantity. Over the years, pressure has been placed on administrators to produce high scores on standardized tests. This has caused a frenzy because administrators are compelled to justify low scores and articulate what they are going to do differently to get better results. It encourages dog-and-pony shows to pacify district leaders, parents, and the community. It's a way to create the illusion of progress, when in truth there is a lot of insignificant work going on that will not contribute to student success. A whole lot of nothing is not the answer.

Quality over quantity should always be the focus when implementing new strategies to meet standards. The saying "less is more" holds true in education. Quality and substance over quantity and shallowness produce the best outcomes. Always doing more is not sustainable, so educators need to be thoughtful about the changes they commit to implementing. Furthermore, focusing on too many things at once can be overwhelming for teachers and staff and can compromise their ability to be effective. Quality work at the school site is more impactful and increases the likelihood of achieving the best results, both in terms of the broader educational goals and providing students with an excellent education.

Creating quality schools can be challenging, especially given the bureaucratic system of operations inherent in the public education sector. Districts and schools need elasticity, not bureaucracy, to advance organically. When leaders in education are bound to bureaucratic structure, creativity is stifled, causing morale and other emotions to take a negative turn. This rigidness also prevents educational practices from evolving with the social climate and technological advances. Bureaucratic practices work against vitality because schools get hung up on past or present successes and/or failures. Regardless of the situation, looking in the rearview mirror perpetuates stagnation. Moving forward towards vitality is essential to the ongoing success in schools.

In order for vitality to be incorporated into the fabric of school practices, educational leaders must include long-term strategic planning, technological advancements, adaptability, awareness of the political climate, and a quality vs. quantity approach in the conversation when planning and setting goals.

Purpose-Driven

Over the past 25 years, I have gained a lot of knowledge and wisdom about education and the operations of schools, and I feel obligated and honored to share what I've learned. I am confident that the more schools we have that are effective, the greater impact education will have on society.

It is so important for educators to reveal what they have learned to be best practices. Educators who are purpose-driven have an innate ability to learn and teach. They are eager to collaborate and share their experiences and knowledge. The more intentional educators become in their practice, the greater the impact they will have on the educational community. The process of building great schools and strengthening education as a whole is a collective effort. We have to continuously work together to get better. There are always trials to overcome. It is an uphill battle, but the ability to overcome obstacles and get to the peak will allow educators to reap the intangible rewards that await those who are committed. The view from the top is amazing and exhilarating. Purpose-driven educators are not deterred by roadblocks or challenges, and they do not give up on the mission—they persevere.

The Purpose-Driven School was written in response to a need to examine education through a fresh lens. The future of humanity and our world is at the mercy of our schools. The education of our youth defines the continued success of our country. This reality places a huge responsibility on schools and educators to educate with excellence and provide all students with a quality education. *The Purpose-Driven School* was written to aid educational leaders in their quest to design quality schools, and the content of these pages includes information and practical applications to further that goal. This book will help good schools transition to great and will help resuscitate schools that are failing or have lost momentum. Foundational and fundamental principles that will support school vitality are presented in this text. School vitality should be the ultimate goal for educators, parents, politicians, and the community. Implementing policies and practices that build vitality should be the goal for educational leaders. What vitality looks like changes with the times, and it is imperative that leaders of the profession have the ability to predict and adapt to shifts in education.

In addition to vitality, this book also discusses the importance vision plays in the success of a school. It includes best practices and procedures to follow when hiring that will lead to constructing the ideal educational team, holistic leadership, and a view of education as a business that provides a service. It also takes a look at the importance of the partnership a teacher has with parents and students. The final thoughts of the book address the achievement gap and effects the 2020 COVID-19 pandemic has had on education and how equity is the leading force in the evolution of educational reform and the progress of humanity.

Ultimately, this book was written to spark an educational movement led by current and next generation leaders who have been called to create change in the educational system and practices. This book will provide educational leaders of today and tomorrow with strategies and common-sense practices that will stand the test of time. Anyone who is invested in the future of America should read this book (educators, community leaders, politicians, parents, corporate leaders, etc.). Quality education is the missing link to eradicating social ills and making the world thrive. Education shapes our future, so we cannot afford to lose sight of its impact on humanity. The social and political climate is calling for change and serving our youth through education is a social justice that must be a priority. Acting as guardians of our youth, educators are in a unique position to lead the charge. As we move forward toward creating quality schools, we must always begin with a *love for all children.*

CHAPTER SUMMARY

- Education is essential to preserving the ecosystem of humanity.

- In a changing world, education will support the advancement of mankind, racial accord, technology, and effective communication.

- To ensure that the world is progressing year after year, schools need the tools to create and maintain vitality.

- Vitality requires an intentional effort to support the immediate and future success of schools, which is predicated on high academic performance of *all students*.

- Vitality in schools requires leaders to be progressive thinkers.

- Factors that schools need to consider when building vitality are long-term strategic planning, technological advancements, adaptability, the changing political climate, and an ongoing commitment to quality.

- Future planning is the bedrock of establishing vitality in schools.

- Technology facilitates the discovery and application of knowledge.

- It is imperative that students are provided with the resources, accessibility, knowledge, and skills to keep pace with technological advancements and are academically and socially relevant.

- For students to maintain a high level of technological expertise, teachers must incorporate technology in their instructional practices.

- Anticipating current and future technological advancements is fundamental to providing students with a quality education.

- Political leaders have a huge influence on education. Keeping a pulse on the political climate allows educators to navigate the implementation of educational policies.

- It is important to focus on quality over quantity when implementing new practices.

- Educational bureaucracy impedes the flexibility that districts and schools need to advance organically.

- Quality education is essential to eradicating social ills and making the world thrive.

PART 1
INFRASTRUCTURE

Building Capacity

CHAPTER 1

Vision

The Foundation for Great Schools

"Where there is no vision, the people perish..."
—PROVERBS 29:18, KJV

Everything that we have on earth started from a vision. When God created the earth, He created it from a vision. All of the best inventions were first visions in someone's mind, either a solution to a problem or anticipation of a future necessity or circumstance.

Think about the airplane. The invention of the airplane allowed people to travel great distances in a short amount of time. This invention changed transportation and the quality of life that we currently enjoy. Not only are humans able to travel great distances with relative ease, transportation of goods and services has improved drastically. The Wright Brothers were credited with being the first to invent, build, and fly an airplane. Orville and Wilbur Wright believed in something that seemed unachievable given the law of gravity. They challenged conventional wisdom and pursued an idea that most people thought impossible. Visions that have the greatest impact on society exceed our wildest imaginations.

Education requires that same creative thought. A school's vision should be equally ambitious, innovative, grand, and forward-thinking, challenging the status quo by pushing beyond perceived limits.

Students deserve the very best, and it is up to educators to envision a superlative educational experience for them. At every level, a student's education should positively impact their future and, in turn, the world.

Vision Is a Destination

When educational leaders have a clear vision of where they would like to arrive, it's time to devise a road map with step-by-step directions to accomplishing the goal. In education, or any other business, the road map is the strategic plan that leads to the vision.

The Wright Brothers wanted to propel an airplane. Once they knew the outcome they wanted to achieve, they identified all of the components needed to actualize the goal. They methodically tackled design, construction, and materials, while building the engine, propellers, and transmission, among focusing on the many other details critical to the success of their invention. The Wright Brothers then coordinated all of the key components to build and power an airplane. Based on their desired outcome, they took the necessary steps to align each component that would lead to actualizing the goal.

Similarly, educational leaders must follow a path that leads to the ultimate vision or destination. A compelling vision motivates all stakeholders, including students, on the journey. When there is a clear vision, any steps off course are apparent. The certainty of the vision pulls educators back on course, which is especially important when the road becomes rocky.

Validity of a Vision

People who are driven by purpose and passion will be challenged on the route to bringing their vision to fruition. These challenges test the sincerity of the vision and the steps that need to be taken. Tests and roadblocks that are so discouraging that they persuade visionaries to abort the mission speak to the validity of the commitment and passion toward the vision.

The world learned about the work and accomplishments of the Wright Brothers, and history accounts their voyage in revolutionizing aviation. As amazing as their invention was and still is, the road to its discovery did not come without challenges. Wilbur and Orville had a lot of trials, and even failures, that tested their commitment to the vision. Despite it all, the Wright Brothers pushed forward. They used their failures to inform the decisions that led to their ultimate success.

A school's vision will be tested. The path to achieving the vision will not be a straight line. There will be twists and turns, bumps and bruises that will seem to inhibit the progress. Educational leaders have to push past any challenges, opposition, or perceived roadblocks and use these difficulties to grow and get better. Barriers provide information to guide or redirect toward the vision. The obstacles on the way to the vision ultimately assess the commitment of the educators to the vision. If failures discourage educators, that will reveal their lack of faithfulness to the vision—and possibly education. Dedication to education and a steadfast commitment to making progress toward the vision are integral in achieving the goal of creating a great school.

Where There Is No Shared Vision, the People Perish

A crucial component to realizing a school's vision is the team. All members of the educational leadership team (which includes all staff members), parents, and the community need to believe in the vision of the school and work relentlessly toward the goal because "where there is no shared vision, the people perish."

As a general rule, schools have a written mission and vision, but is there a team of individuals to back up that vision and actively work toward achieving the ultimate goal? Oftentimes, the educational community is not familiar with the mission and vision of the school, and these gaps compromise the potential of success. A starting point includes communicating the vision to the school's stakeholders to merge or solidify the shared vision.

A vision is simply a dream if there are no actions to substantiate it. The vision of schools and education as a whole have to be active and impactful in order to affect change on a global scale. Education is a vehicle to support the development and evolution of civilization and humanity. All schools need stakeholders invested in the vision in order to maximize their influence on society. The success of a school is compromised when there is not a shared vision. When parents, districts, and school leaders do not have a shared vision, low-performing schools are inevitable. It is only when the school community supports the vision that vitality can exist.

Vision and Vitality

Vision is directly rooted in vitality. The first airplane model that the Wright Brothers built in 1903 was wildly different from the planes we rely on today. Planes have evolved in size and scope to serve a variety of purposes and to assist in global advancement. Over the years, engineers have ensured that the Wright Brothers' invention has maintained its vitality by progressing aviation and staying relevant with the current travel and transportation needs, helping society advance. The aviation industry continues to create vitality through a commitment to purposeful and relevant existence.

Schools are charged with the same task of sustaining vitality. Schools must start with a vision and lay out a plan that is forward-thinking in its implementation. A school's vision should be active and not static. The vision must consider the longevity of its impact and its ability to evolve with the current and future social, political, and economic climate. A good educational vision must be innovative and progressive.

Conclusion

Nothing happens without vision; it is the cornerstone to achieving any goal. Having a vision sets an intention for future goals and desired results. In order for any outcome to manifest, it must be first conceived in the mind. This is why vision is the necessary first step to building a foundation for creating and maintaining great schools.

Visions are inspired by a need, a passion, or a purpose. Education encompasses all three. There is a need, and those who are drawn to education have been pulled there by their passion and purpose. Educators should have a vision to positively impact the lives of students, a vision that creates the architectural blueprint for purpose.

Operating a school without a vision is a recipe for disaster. All stakeholders should know and understand the mission and vision of the school. That is a basic requirement, and as simple as it is, it can have a huge impact. Actions then must follow in order to meet the desired end. A school's vision has to be thoughtful and reflect the long-term results of student success. The projection of student success allows educational leaders to design and implement progressive goals that will lead to the larger vision. In education, the key to implementing and successfully fulfilling a vision is having the right team.

CHAPTER SUMMARY

- Everything on earth started from a vision!
- Visions are either a solution to a problem or answers to a future necessity or circumstance.
- *All students* deserve the very best, and it is up to educators to envision a superlative educational experience for them. Education at every level should have a positive impact on their future and, in turn, the world.
- When educational leaders have a clear vision of where they would like to arrive, a road map can assist in getting to the ultimate destination.
- People who are driven by purpose will be challenged on their journey to bring their vision to fruition. These challenges will test the sincerity of the vision and guide or redirect toward the vision.
- Operating a school without a vision is a recipe for disaster.
- Vision is compromised when it is not shared by the parents, districts, and school leaders.
- The vision must consider the longevity of its impact and its ability to evolve with the current and future social, political, and economic climate.
- A school's vision has to be thoughtful and reflect the long-term results of student success.
- A solid vision has to be the first stepping-stone to building vitality in a school. Having a vision sets an intention for future goals and desired results.
- A team of visionaries is a critical component to realizing the vision of a school.

CHAPTER 2

Dream Team

Teamwork Makes the Dream Work

"The strength of the team is each individual member.
The strength of each member is the team."

—PHIL JACKSON,
former NBA basketball player, coach, and executive

The 1992 Summer Olympics held in Barcelona, Spain, hosted a memorable USA Men's Basketball team, thought to be the best sports team ever constructed. Prior to 1992, Olympic teams consisted of amateur basketball players, which made it difficult for the USA to bring home the gold medal. After much debate, the International Basketball Federation (FIBA) decided that professional players were eligible to play on the Olympic team. The USA Olympic team promptly turned its attention to the National Basketball Association (NBA) to create an incredible team capable of winning gold. Not only did the team show up and take the gold, they showed off. They played games that amazed the audience and their opponents alike. In Barcelona, there was a huge amount of respect for the USA players and the strategic game they played. The 1992 USA Men's Olympic Basketball team consisted of NBA icons: Michael Jordan, Magic Johnson, Larry Bird, Charles Barkley, Karl Malone, John Stockton, Patrick Ewing, David Robinson, Clyde Drexler, Scottie Pippen, Chris Mullin, and Christian Laettner. It's no wonder they were dubbed the "Dream Team."

The Dream Team

Putting together an educational Dream Team is critical to successfully implementing and achieving a school's vision. This team includes *everyone* who works for the school (i.e., administrators, teachers, paraprofessionals, custodial and support staff, etc.) and volunteers. Given the supreme importance of implementing and fulfilling the school's mission and vision, creating an educational Dream Team has to be a top priority. The process of assembling the Dream Team requires an intentional, systematic approach during the selection process. When the USA Olympic Basketball team was created, the NBA chose professional athletes who were the best of the best. In order to design and implement the optimal educational program, seeking and hiring consummate professionals must be the goal. When I speak about professionals, I am referring to individuals who work in any given position and who perform at a high level of standard in that position. They possess unique qualities and have a superior work ethic.

Qualities of a high-performing professional:
- disciplined
- self-confident
- self-motivated
- problem-solver
- organized
- team player
- strong desire to succeed
- positive attitude
- growth mindset
- excellent attendance and punctuality

- courageous
- innovative
- natural-born leader
- reflect on their practice
- optimistic

What was so great about the USA Olympic Dream Team was not so much their individual talent, but how they used their individual talent in support of the team's goal. The success of the team became their personal goal. What made them amazing was their passion for the game and their desire to win.

That same philosophy has to be considered when seeking and building an educational Dream Team, and this begins with a vision. Having a clear vision helps to guide in selecting the right members of the team. When developing the vision for the team, there has to be consideration for the desired culture and climate—the energy that will resonate on the campus. Establishing a positive culture is necessary to achieving the mission of the school. Passion for education and a wish to work with a diverse group of students is a must for individuals being considered for the Dream Team. Most importantly, a school needs individuals who will add value to the program.

In every successful business or organization, you will find a group of leaders working together toward a common goal. When I decided to open Rosebud Academy, I knew that it was going to be critical to hire a group of leaders who believed in what I was doing, who had a positive attitude, and who were self-motivated to be successful in the work that they do.

The first teacher I hired was a former student of mine from when I taught 8th grade. I knew that she was the perfect candidate because of the qualities she possessed as a student. She was a conscientious student who worked hard and was self-motivated to perform well. Unfortunately, we do not always get to know people before we hire them, which was the case with the second teacher I hired. I interviewed her and I even had an opportunity to observe her teaching in class. During the classroom observation, she had excellent command over the class, great classroom management skills, and she knew the content of the subjects she was teaching. She even performed well during her interview. I was impressed and felt confident about offering her the job. Everything was perfect. I had hired what I thought to be the two teachers that I needed to open the school.

Prior to school starting I started to see some red flags. The second teacher I hired was quite vocal and combative when it came to implementing the curriculum and challenging students. As I expressed that teaching academic vocabulary to the students was an important part of their instruction, this teacher became frustrated and said she didn't feel the need to teach students words that they were not going to use in their everyday lives. I explained why it was important for students to learn academic vocabulary and reminded her of the mission and vision for the students. Over the course of the school year, this teacher continued to communicate that she was not in agreement with the school's vision and the implementation of the instructional practices. It became evident that this was not a perfect match.

Selecting the Dream Team: Recruiting and Hiring

Hiring the right people can be an overwhelming task. There is a certain mindset that has to emerge for the individuals who are doing the hiring—a mindset that taps into all of the senses. This allows the interviewer to use their instinct, common sense, knowledge, and experiences to narrow down the candidates and identify the ideal employee. Understanding how to tap into these faculties will help unlock the intellect needed to fully engage in the recruiting and hiring process in a way that actively supports the hiring vision and goals. There is definitely a method to the madness when it comes to hiring.

The process of hiring is like online dating. With online dating, you have two individuals who want to connect with their soul mate or someone with whom they are compatible. Like these two online daters, the employer is looking for the perfect employee to fill a position, and the potential employee is seeking the perfect job. In education, the employer is looking for someone who meets the requirements and has the educational credentials or certificates that are necessary to fill the position. In addition to their credentials or education, an employer is looking for certain personality traits or characteristics that are compatible for the position and the school culture. The candidate is looking for the ideal school where they can thrive and be happy. So, let's call educational hiring EduHarmony.

EduHarmony is the practice of connecting the right employees with the right employer in the profession of education. The process of an employer and employee finding each other begins with a search. Anyone who registers for a dating website or app has to complete a questionnaire that includes a list of qualities they are looking for in a mate. The dating site will also ask a series of questions to see if other clients possess the qualities that they are seeking. Another part of the process for online dating is attaching a photo to the profile. The photo will allow potential mates to choose someone who is also visually appealing or attractive according to their standards. If the vetting process checks out, they will meet in person for a first date. This same process occurs with educational hiring. The employer places an ad online advertising the position for which they are hiring. In that advertisement, there is a profile that describes the position and the duties for the job. It also outlines the requirements needed to qualify for the position and the desired qualifications and skills. Individuals who are looking for employment will search online for jobs that are a potential good fit. These potential employees will read the profile of the position and determine if they possess those qualifications. If they meet the qualifications and are interested in the position, they will submit an application and résumé. The two parties have connected by showing interest in one another. The employer is then charged with the task of reviewing all of the applications, résumés, and letters of recommendation—gathering information from the documentation received.

The process of selecting the best possible mate, or employee in this case, will begin with viewing the candidate's profile or checking their credentials to see if they meet the minimum requirements for the position. Reviewing the applications and letters of recommendation will allow an employer to see which applicants qualify for the position. Through that process the search is narrowed down. Those who have passed the initial phase of meeting the minimum requirements will be contacted, and the interview process will begin. The interviewing process usually involves a phone call or maybe an email to set up "the date," or in employment terms, "the interview." When the two strangers meet, they hope to feel chemistry. In dating, chemistry is a physical connection. In a job interview, chemistry is an energetic field connection felt by the employer and the potential employee. It is nonverbal and it allows an interviewer to ascertain if the interviewee possesses the right chemistry to create the dynamics necessary to build a Dream Team. The interview should be likened to a first date. When interviewing a candidate, there should be a chemical reaction during the face-to-face interaction and fielding questions.

Having the right people on an educational Dream Team is critical. Therefore, the next several sections offer specific details on the hiring process, as intentionality is key when finding the best candidate. Absorbing the mental, emotional, and energetic sequencing and processes involved in selecting members of an educational team will make the hiring process flow smoothly.

The Application

Employment applications are the starting point for selecting the best possible candidates for an open position. Every part of the employment application informs the employer, and the application can be used as an opportunity to begin getting to know the applicant. There should be a focus on the details, starting with where the applicant lives in respect to the school. Consideration should be given to how far the candidate would have to commute to work daily and whether that will be a factor in the decision to hire. A long commute could affect punctuality or attendance and might also lead to burnout. Depending on what position is being filled, the candidate's level of education is important. Do they possess a high school diploma? When did they graduate from high school? The educational background and credentials need to be assessed for certificated employees. As employers read through the application, questions for the applicant should be formulated to help fill in the gaps from the information gathered reading the application.

Reading the application should be deliberate and detailed. The goal should be to gain pre-knowledge about the applicant and to help determine if the applicant qualifies for a spot on the Dream Team. Employment history provides extremely valuable information about the work commitment of the applicant. If an applicant has an employment history that reflects several jobs worked for one year or less, that is a red flag. It makes a statement about their personality, commitment, and work ethic. Whether or not the applicant has a criminal history is critical to the hiring process. Do not overlook this part of the process. There is power in the application. It sets the foundation for the interview and assists in defining personality traits. If the goal is to create a great school, hiring has to be taken very seriously. Hiring to just have a warm body will be detrimental to achieving the mission and vision of the school.

Letters of Reference

The letters of reference complement the application and help the employer fill out the profile of the applicant and put the pieces of the puzzle together. Reference letters divulge information about the applicant's work ethic, reliability, competence, passion, and commitment both to education and the position for which they are applying. No matter what position is being filled, finding a team of like-minded individuals who are working toward the mission and vision of the school is the ultimate goal.

When reviewing letters of reference, there needs to be consideration for who wrote the letter. A good applicant will have a letter from their current or last supervisor. Individuals who have just graduated from college should have a letter of recommendation from a professor and a supervising teacher from their student teaching practice. Ideally, letters of recommendation serve as the voice of someone who knows the applicant's character and has experienced their work ethic. The individuals who write the letters of recommendation should speak from the heart and send the reader a message.

The length and detail of the letter conveys the author's commitment to the candidate and the extent of their relationship. A short, general letter communicates one or more of the following:

1. The author does not know the applicant well.

2. The applicant has not left a lasting, positive impression on the author.

3. The author wrote the letter out of obligation, and they likely couldn't say no.

Consider the details of the letter and the word choices used to describe the candidate. A letter of recommendation that is thoughtful and has specific details communicates to the reader: I know this applicant, I believe in this applicant, and I vouch for this applicant. A best practice is to read the recommendation letters twice and take notes. Creating a picture of and profile for each applicant allows the employer to maximize their potential to hire the best employee for the position (see Dream Team Reflection Form later in this chapter).

The Interview

Going into the interview prepared is extremely important for the interviewer. The employer should have created a profile for all of the applicants. (Note: There are some applicants who should not make it to the interview based on the information ascertained from the application and recommendations.) While each profile is in development, a list of questions should be generated while reading the application, résumé, and letters of recommendation to ask during the interview. There should also be standard questions that are asked to each candidate in addition to these applicant-specific questions. The interview is extremely important; therefore, preparedness and intention have to be a huge priority.

Interview Questions

There are two levels of interview questions that should be considered when hiring. The first level is *leading interview questions*, or primary interview questions. Leading interview questions are the questions created based on the information found or not found in the application, résumé, and letters of recommendation. These queries are specific questions related to the candidates. They will help the employer learn more about the applicant and will fill in any gaps. These questions will help to create a personality profile. Once a candidate meets all of the minimum requirements for the position, learning more about their personality will help determine how well they will fit in with the culture of the school.

Fundamental interview questions are generic questions that an employer asks all potential employees. These secondary questions help to establish how well a candidate will perform in a position. The answers to these questions will communicate how passionate they are about education as well as the strength of their critical-thinking and communication skills. They will also give an employer insight into a potential candidate's philosophy on education and will determine if they believe in the school's vision. Secondary questions will solidify the personality profile. These questions will sometimes cross over into primary questions if they become relevant to the development of the profile in the application, résumé, and letters of recommendation review. Both levels of questioning are important to the interview process no matter how they are categorized. The intention will define each question's role in the process (see sample interview questions later in this chapter).

Face-to-Face Dynamics

When the interviewee walks into the room, an employer should be receiving information. The first impression is the last impression—meaning, the appearance and confidence of the applicant provides valuable, lasting information about the person's personality, mental state, etc. An employer should be constantly assessing the potential employee during the interview. If they show up to the interview late, that is a *deal breaker*! From the time the applicant walks in, an employer can instinctively categorize him or her as a good candidate, potentially good candidate, or not a fit.

As the interview progresses, the questions asked are a strategic attempt to learn more about the applicant, establish if they are qualified, and determine if their thoughts align with the school's mission and vision. Another quality an employer should look for in an applicant is their ability to adapt. Hiring someone who has an aversion to learning and growing could be detrimental to the progress of the school. Education is always evolving, and the school's leaders' ability to adapt without resistance will dictate the success of the school.

Once the interview concludes, time should be taken to jot down notes about the applicant (pros and cons, etc.). There should be a standard format used to rate and rank all applicants. The process of interviewing should be organized and systematic. It is important for employers to be prepared for the interview and to keep track of the information regarding each employee. When interviewing several candidates, it is difficult to keep track of everyone without notes that reference what was learned about the interviewee during the interview. Rating each candidate will help to narrow down the search. Once the pool has been narrowed down to half of those interviewed, a call to the top candidates should be made for a second interview (see Dream Team Reflection Form later in this chapter).

Interview Tips:

- It is ideal to have more than one interviewer present. This will create an opportunity to compare notes afterwards. Multiple interviewers will help to confirm or validate observations.

- Steer away from hiring someone who needs to be micro-managed because they will likely derail the mission of the team.

- Hire people with instinct, those who take the initiative to fill a need.

- Individuals who are going to add value to the school's program are the best for the team. The DREAM TEAM!

Sample Leading Interview Questions/Primary Interview Questions

1. How did you learn of this position?

2. If hired, would you commute to work or would you relocate?

3. What made you move to this area? (if they moved from another state or area)

4. What degrees, certificates, and educational experience do you have? (if needed for the position)

5. What work experience do you have as it relates to the position you're applying for?

6. Explain the gaps in your employment history.

7. Based on your employment history, you haven't stayed at a job past a year. Is there a reason for the brevity in your employment relations?

8. Do you plan on continuing your education beyond your associate's or bachelor's degree?

9. Work history questions that come to mind while reading the application and résumé.

10. Questions regarding information that was learned or not revealed about the applicant from the application, résumé, or letters of recommendation.

Sample Fundamental Interview Questions/Secondary Interview Questions

1. Tell me about yourself.

2. Why did you apply for this position?

3. What made you enter the field of education?

4. What is your educational philosophy?

5. What are some of your strengths?

6. In what areas would you like to improve?

7. When you were in school, what was your favorite subject?

8. What academic subjects do you enjoy teaching most?

9. What are you passionate about?

10. Would you describe yourself as being an organized person? Explain.

11. What is your idea of high standards?

12. Describe your classroom ecology.

13. How would you prepare to start as a first-year teacher?

14. How would you connect with students in an effort to maximize student engagement?

15. How do you feel your education has prepared you for teaching in the classroom?

16. How would you diffuse a conflict between students?

17. How would you mediate a conflict between two students?

18. How would you communicate with a parent about a situation that happened during recess?

19. Describe a time when you had to adapt to a situation.

20. What unique skills do you bring to the table?

21. How strong are your technology skills? How would you use technology in the classroom?

22. What attracted you to this school?

23. What do you know about our school?

24. Why did you leave your last job? Why do you want to leave your current job?

25. What did you like least about your last job?

26. What did you like most about your last job?

27. What would your last/current employer say about you?

28. What have you learned from your previous employment that will help you on this job?

29. What are your priorities and intentions for working at this school site?

30. How would you describe or define teamwork?

31. If working with children of color: Do you have any racial biases that would prevent you from educating the students at a level that will support their long-term success or incline you to treat them unfairly?

32. What added value do you think you can bring to the team/school?

33. What characteristics are you looking for in a school site?

34. What is your availability?

35. Do you have any questions for me?

Second Interview/Follow-Up Questions

1. What do you like about working with children?

2. What have you learned about children by working with them?

3. How have you grown by working with children?

4. How would you prepare students emotionally and academically for high school or college?

5. What motivates you?

6. What are you passionate about?

7. What are your professional goals?

8. Where do you see yourself in 5 years?

9. Where do you see yourself in 10 years?

10. What has been your greatest accomplishment?

11. Describe good customer service.

12. What has been the most rewarding experience of your career so far?

13. How would you handle an irate parent?

14. How do you handle stress?

15. What is your salary range expectation?

16. Why should I hire you?

Personal Connection Interview Questions

1. If you could travel anywhere in the world, where would it be?

2. What is the best book you have read, and why? What book do you feel everyone should read?

Making a personal connection with the employee candidate is important when trying to attract the best applicant for the Dream Team. Make an intentional effort to tailor personal connection questions to each candidate. Use the information you have learned about them in the process to get to know who they are personally and to connect with them on a deeper level. Connection is everything when bringing the right people together.

Note: Any interview questions not asked in the first interview can be asked during the second interview.

Follow-up email sent: _____   Overall rating: _____

Denial email sent: _____   2nd interview: _____

Dream Team Reflection Form

Applicant's Name: _____

Position: _____

Rate the applicant based on application and letter of recommendation (circle one): 1 2 3 4 5
Questions you want to ask applicant based on application and letter of recommendation (note the candidate's answers to questions in the interview):

Question:

Response:

Question:

Response:

Question:

Response:

Question:

Response:

Concerns: _____

Rate the applicant following the interview (circle one):
1 2 3 4 5
Candidate will be called back for a second interview: Yes / No
_____ Candidate is not qualified or appropriate for this position.

Notes:

Chemical Reaction

There is a culture that is created by the chemistry of the staff. When the chemistry is off, so too will be the road to achieving the vision of the school. A lack of chemistry is not only awkward, it also impedes the ability to build the dynamics necessary to operate as a Dream Team.

To see if there is the right chemistry, the interview needs to be conversational. As much as an employer wants to find the perfect match for the position, the interviewee is also looking for the perfect school. Good employees will have more options and opportunities presented to them. They will be looking for something beyond the position itself when selecting a school. Most likely, the interviewee will have submitted several applications to different districts or schools. So, making the school desirable is of high importance to attracting good candidates. Finding ways to connect with the interviewee will make working at the school appealing to them. If there is anything that can be added to connect with the interviewee, include that in the dialogue. For example, if a personal connection can be made through a shared hobby, like yoga, briefly discuss this common interest in the interview. You want the connection and selection to be mutual. The goal is to find the perfect chemistry for the team, so there must be an exchange.

Communicating with the applicant about the school's vision, demographics, culture, and climate is important to finding the perfect match. Providing them with a bird's-eye view of the school environment in which they will work will allow them to determine if they fit in with what has been created. The last thing you want is to hire someone who does not believe in the school's vision or has a different philosophy about education than school leaders and parents. Having someone on the team whose educational philosophy is not in alignment with the mission and vision of the school will disrupt the efforts of the team to reach the ultimate goals. For example, if the school's culture and mission involve not assigning students homework, finding out if the candidate also believes in not assigning homework will avoid hiring someone who is not compatible for the school. Addressing this is necessary; otherwise, you will hire the wrong person and spin your wheels trying to fit a square peg into a round hole.

As administrators go through the application and interviewing process, they must keep in mind that it is important for the applicant to be passionate about education. Passion cannot be taught or learned. It is, however, possible to train and coach someone who is passionate and eager to learn how to do a good job.

When hiring for non-teaching positions, the goal is to hire someone who believes in education and the vision for the school. Find out how they can contribute to the school's goals, mission, and vision in their desired position.

Recruiting and Hiring Checklist

- Create a detailed job description, mandatory qualifications, and desired qualities and qualifications.

- Post the job in the appropriate web listing for school positions and attend college job fairs. Request letters of recommendation and résumés with the application.

- Collect applications, résumés, and letters of recommendation in an organized fashion (alphabetical, by qualifications, etc.).

- Review all applications, résumés, and letters of recommendation with details. Take notes.

- Prioritize candidates according to how they rank. (Use the Dream Team Reflection Form.)

- Schedule first interviews.

- Create a chart with dates and times of scheduled interviews. The chart should include the names of candidates and any pertinent information about the candidate.

- Allow 30 minutes–1 hour for each interview and 30 minutes to debrief after each interview. Schedule interviews every 1 hour–90 minutes, if scheduled back-to-back.

- Narrow down the interviewed candidates to your top candidates. (Again, use the Dream Team Reflection Form.)
- Schedule a second interview for top candidates.
- Make a decision and make an offer.
- Once the offer is accepted, send a respectful and encouraging denial letter/email to applicants who were not selected.

The Honeymoon Phase

An individual is hired based on their qualifications, the letters of recommendation, and the interview—a process that is likened to the courting period. The marriage proposal comes when the candidate is offered an employment opportunity. If they accept the proposal and they are hired, they get an engagement ring. They start work when the paperwork is completed and the background check is cleared. Once they start work, they are married. The honeymoon period lasts six months to a year. During this time, the new employee's personality characteristics are discovered, along with how capable they are of doing the job and how well they fit into the school's culture. During the honeymoon period, it may turn out that the relationship will not work out. If the person hired is ineffective at the position they were hired for, a divorce is in order. Releasing the individual from the position is imperative. If they are not in sync with the team, they will impede the progress—and that is a deal breaker. It is possible to hire someone who is not quite up to par but still has potential. Like relationships, with good communication and a serious effort to work toward strengthening the relationship or job, it is worth continuing to develop and grow.

The Symphony: Making Beautiful Music

Ultimately, a school's success will come down to the coordinated efforts of everyone on the team. The staff has to feel the work that they do both in body and spirit. The school's mission is the heartbeat, reflected in the pulse that reaches from head to toe. This synchronicity makes the day-to-day operations come alive. The school's culture breathes and works in conjunction with the heartbeat. The staff members must operate and function in sync with the school's heartbeat, in perfect tempo, just as dance partners have to coordinate their steps and constantly be on the same beat to successfully perform the dance routine. If one person is off beat, there will be a disruption in the flow of the routine. The strength of the school will be found in the rhythm of its staff, parents, and students. Disharmony impedes progress towards the mission and vision. Any organization, corporation, business, or group that can find the rhythm will be successful.

A prime example of a business that has managed to make beautiful music in its day-to-day operations is a local fast-food restaurant, Chick-fil-A. The drive-through reflects the pace necessary to run a successful business. There are two lines when you first enter the drive-through. There are anywhere from 4 to 6 employees taking orders, depending on the length of the line. There is an unspoken flow for moving from car to car. There is an unrehearsed synchronicity that exists among the employees. After cars have ordered and continue to move through the line, the lanes merge and the cars take turns flowing into a single lane. I have yet to see a car merge out of order. There is something about the structure and flow—the rhythm that everyone feels—that creates harmony and makes the restaurant successful. The long lines move systematically and methodically. Payment is taken in the process of moving in the line. When you get to the window, they greet you by your name and your food is ready. That is why no one minds the long lines—because they are confident that it is going to flow and move swiftly. The service is excellent, and the employees are friendly and professional. That is the culture and standard of the business. I am always fascinated by this restaurant. They are consistent in their delivery of excellent customer service. When I am in the drive-through, I hear the symphony playing as I watch the flow of the operation. It's like music to my ears. They work together to reduce the energy that everyone has to put forth. They know they are better together. The success of the overall mission is predicated on the rhythm they create as a team. Anyone who is not in harmony with the team will slow down the process.

The heart of educating students requires an upbeat rhythm. In order for educational leaders to create beautiful music, they have to hear the same song and move on the same beat. When hiring, the goal is to create or maintain the rhythm of the school. In order to be in tune, all employees have to harmonize. When all employees approach their role with an ear to the heartbeat of the school, a passion for education, and abundant love for *all children*, beautiful music will always be made.

Racial Equality

Schools must be filled with educators who have let down their guard with respect to race and racial equality. Systematic racial inequality is prevalent in schools and these inequalities are perpetuated by educators. The hiring process has to address potential employees' sentiment toward race and educating students of color. Until recently, racial biases have been hidden behind masks of innocence. The unveiling of systematic racism has sent shock waves across the nation. However, the revelation that racism still exists in America comes as no surprise to educators, students, and parents who have experienced it firsthand.

Schools are facilitators of racism, and educational leaders have a responsibility to eradicate racism and racial biases in schools. In order to do so, those difficult conversations need to happen. From there, education must be used as a vehicle to level the playing field for students of color. Hiring practices should consider and prevent racism in schools. The educational team is a part of the solution and whoever is hired must be tuned into the sensitive nature of racial biases. If the potential candidate is uncomfortable or uneasy with the subject of race and racism, that fact alone speaks volumes. They are most likely not ready for change and equality. Education cannot afford to continue to grant approval to educational leaders who are not willing to be a part of the process of change.

Schools have an obligation to work toward dismantling racism in education. This work is not solely for public schools that serve a large percentage of students of color. It is also for schools where there is not diversity, including private and parochial schools, and schools that serve homogenous student populations. The issue of racism and inequity affects everyone who does not fit the description of heterosexual, white, male, and affluent. This push toward equity and access enfolds all those who sit in the margins of the dominant culture. The goal is to remove hate and discrimination toward any group of people, but it will take the work of everyone.

Retaining Good Employees

Hiring good employees is one thing; retaining them is another. Retaining your Dream Team is the key to building long-term success. Education is a calling, and the majority of people who enter the field, in any capacity, have a passion for what they do. When people are driven by their passion, they already possess the intrinsic motivation and drive to do what they do. Retaining employees largely depends on external factors that can be built into the school culture.

As a starting point, good employees have a positive attitude, and they want to be around other positive people. Creating and preserving an enthusiastic school culture is the first step in retaining good employees. The school environment is made dynamic when team members are positive, kind, and collaborative. The work environment is a big part of a person's life—and feeling good about the relationships one has with their colleagues is a huge bonus. Employers who provide a shared goal and vision to unite behind create a magical atmosphere. A friendly and collegial environment will go a long way to attract and keep an employee. Additional considerations for retention include:

- Respect
- Supportive and collaborative environment
- Leadership opportunities
- Mentoring program
- Clean work environment
- Up-to-date educational technology
- Access to necessary supplies
- Appreciation/gratitude/celebrations
- Rapport
- Autonomy
- Transparency
- Shared decision-making
- Trust

Conclusion

Teachers and staff are a school's most precious resource. Investing in education's greatest resource can make the difference between creating ordinary or great schools, simply getting by or truly maximizing student learning. Hiring the right individuals is of extreme importance to fulfilling the mission and vision of the school. Every person hired needs to believe in the vision and mission of the school. The care that goes into hiring and creating an educational Dream Team will drive school vitality. Implementing a hiring process that is thoughtful, procedural, and instinctual will further facilitate good decision-making. Employers must be cognizant of the dual dynamic that creates a positive connection and makes the relationship mutually beneficial. Building a Dream Team is one thing, but retaining these professionals is another. Retaining great employees is critical to building and maintaining great schools. Education is a social issue and the true professional responsibility for authentic educators is in their humanity. Educators have to have the ability to be conscious of racial differences and self-reflect on their own inherent biases in an effort to provide all students with an opportunity to be successful long-term. So, the hiring process has to be purposeful in its endeavors to maximize the ability to hire strong candidates who will become valuable members of the Dream Team.

CHAPTER SUMMARY

- Putting together an educational Dream Team is critical to successfully implementing and achieving the school's vision.

- The educational team includes *everyone* who works for the school (i.e., administrators, teachers, custodians, support staff, paraprofessionals, etc.) and individuals who volunteer regularly.

- In order to design and implement the optimal educational program, you have to seek and hire professionals with a superior work ethic.

- Having a clear vision helps to select the right members of the Dream Team.

- The individuals who are doing the hiring need to tap into all their senses to identify the right candidate.

- In any hiring process, the employer is looking for the perfect employee to fill a position, and the potential employee is looking for the perfect job.

- Employment applications are the starting point for vetting candidates for filling an open position and creating individual profiles.

- The letters of recommendation complement the application, giving the employer an opportunity to add to their profile of the applicant.

- The letters of recommendation should be from someone who knows the applicant and has experienced their work ethic and character.

- A list of questions should be generated while reading the application, résumé, and letters of recommendation to be asked during the interview process.

- There are two levels of interview questions that should be considered when hiring: *leading interview questions* and *fundamental interview questions.*

- *Leading interview questions* are created based on the information found (or not found) in the application, résumé, and letters of recommendation.

- *Fundamental interview questions* are generic questions that an employer asks all potential employees.

- The questions asked during the interview are a strategic attempt to learn more about the applicant, determine if they are qualified, and to see if their thoughts are in alignment with the school's mission and vision.

- There is a culture created by the chemistry of the staff. When the chemistry is off, the vision of the school will be unattainable.

- Good employee candidates will have more options and opportunities presented to them. Create an exchange that makes a personal connection.

- Communicating with the applicant about the school's vision, demographics, culture, and climate is important to finding the perfect match.

- As administrators go through the application and interviewing process, they must assess the applicant's passion for education.

- When hiring for non-teaching positions, find out how the candidate can contribute to the school's goals, mission, and vision in their position.

- In the honeymoon period (the first 6 months to 1 year of employment), a new employee's personality traits are discovered, their ability to do the job is uncovered, and how well they fit into the culture of the school is revealed.

- If it turns out that the person hired is ineffective at the position they were hired for, a termination is in order.

- Ultimately, a school's success will come from the coordinated efforts of everyone on the team.
- When there is disharmony among the staff, parents, and students, it impedes the progress of working toward the school's mission and vision.
- Systemic racial inequality is prevalent in schools, and these inequalities are perpetuated by educators.
- The hiring process has to address potential employees' sentiments toward race and educating students of color.
- More important than hiring the right team, retaining them is the key to building long-term success.
- Employers that unite employees in pursuit of a shared goal create a magical atmosphere.

CHAPTER 3

Leadership

_____

Setting the Example for Excellence

*"If your actions inspire others to dream more, learn more, do more,
and become more, you are a leader."*

—JOHN QUINCY ADAMS, *sixth U.S. president*

A s an educational leader it was important for me to grow
mentally, emotionally, and spiritually. I had to constantly
evolve, through self-reflection, self-awareness, and change.
Understanding that being the best version of myself would encourage other staff to aspire to be the best version of themselves. It was
important for me to lead with compassion, and since everyone
needs to be heard, validated, and filled up, I needed to foster a
sincere, organic, and positive relationship with all the staff. Along
the way, I came to believe that our school community was brought
together for a reason. I decided I wanted to have a positive impact
on those who came into my life, hoping that people felt better off
because of our relationship.

Administrative leaders are responsible for navigating multiple
layers of people, personalities, and processes—each with its own
challenges. The people directly connected to the administrator are
teachers, staff, students, parents, businesses, and the community.
Different administrative roles will deal with each person or group
based on the level of responsibility assigned to the position. This

requires an administrator to wear an array of hats to address the diverse needs of individuals or groups. The people who make up the school community represent a wide range of characteristics, needs, wants, or services. Managing the unique personalities and the different types of relationships takes skill and finesse. Effectively and successfully interacting with all parties associated with a school is a craft that can be learned.

Administrative leaders must connect with employees based on their Individual Employee Personality (IEP). The specific traits or characteristics that show up in the work environment define the employee both personally and professionally. The IEP defines not only who they are, but also what matters to them. Taking the time to get to know an employee's disposition is vital to designing a management and leadership style that fits each employee's identity. Learning employee personalities takes time and patience.

Being a good listener and having good instincts are skills that must be brought to all of the interactions that enable administrative leaders to learn IEPs. Formal and informal observations, conversations, and interactions are also key factors to defining an IEP. Formal conversations and interactions are specifically related to the job—for example, an observation on classroom structure or instructional practice. Informal observations are dialogues and interactions that are not associated with the job. This could be a casual exchange about family or personal life. It could also be a distant observation between two employees that informs personality traits and characteristics. The formal and informal observations paint a picture about who the employee is and what is important to him or her. Using instinct to be in tune to verbal and non-verbal cues is a major component when defining an employee's IEP. Once the IEPs have been identified, all interactions and conversations should be tailored to meet and support their IEP. A continuous effort to get to know each employee is a part of developing sustainable relationships with everyone on the team.

School administrators should have a clear understanding that everyone who works at a school site is part of the leadership team. However, there is a hierarchy of leadership in education. At the school site, the top of the hierarchy is the administration, next is the certificated staff (teachers, counselors, etc.), and then there is the non-certificated staff (teachers' aides, noon staff, recess and lunch staff, after-school staff, custodians, etc.). When dealing with children in the school setting, every employee takes on a leadership role.

Leadership Congruency Postulate

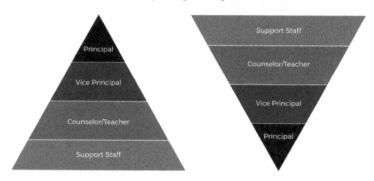

The *Leadership Congruency Postulate* is the idea or understanding that every staff member, regardless of their title, is a leader. The postulate further suggests that the hierarchy of leadership at any given time can be at any level. Each position can hold the highest ranking of power at certain times during the day, week, month, and year. For example, noon aides monitor and support students during lunchtime. While they are on the playground, they are the highest-ranking leader. In the classroom, the teacher is the highest-ranking leader, not the principal. The principal, vice principal, or dean steps into the highest-ranking leader position when a student is sent to the office by the teacher or noon aide for misconduct or any other situation that cannot be resolved by the staff in charge at the time. Administrators also exercise their rank when a teacher or staff member needs help handling a situation with a parent as it relates to a student. Every rank of leadership has a different level of responsibility, but all employees are an integral part of the leadership team and should be respected as a leader at all levels. Each leader needs to be empowered to lead at their level and to perform their duties with pride and dignity.

The Leadership Congruency Postulate is similar to the leadership model found in police departments. There are different ranks in positions. The police rankings from top to bottom can be categorized as follows: chief of police, deputy police chief, police captain, police lieutenant, police sergeant, police corporal, police officer, and police technician. The chief of police is usually the highest rank of authority in the police department, but they entrust decision-making to the other ranking officers in the day-to-day operations. At the station, whoever has the highest rank present is the person in charge. When a decision needs to be made at the scene of a crime, the highest-ranking officer serves as the lead decision maker. If a higher-ranking officer arrives at that same scene, they then become the person in charge.

The Leadership Congruency Postulate is helpful to understanding how leadership in the school setting is fluid, but it is also imperative to distinguish the depth of responsibility at each level of leadership. Typically, the level of responsibility placed on a school employee can be discerned based on their title. The title in and of itself allows staff, parents, students, and community members to address the appropriate person given their questions, concerns, or business.

Oftentimes we look at the levels of leadership as mutually exclusive; however, they are best described as mutually beneficial. Creating vitality in schools involves creating an energy among the leadership team that resonates among all employees and empowers them to leverage their individual skill sets for the greater good of the mission and vision of the school. Everyone who takes on a role as an educational leader needs to acknowledge and accept the weight and prestige of their role.

Utilitarian Doctrine

One of the primary responsibilities of leadership is making decisions. Regardless of how great a school program is, there is always going to be someone who has a complaint or disagrees with decisions being made. No matter how wonderful things are—even if there are kittens, candy, and rainbows involved—it is impossible to please everyone. That is just the nature of the beast, especially in education. In business, the goal is to always please the customer. But in education, when you are dealing with a large group of people, there must be an understanding that you are not going to please everyone. There has to be a rule of thumb to apply when making decisions so that the greatest number of people affected by the decision receives the greatest good.

The Utilitarian Doctrine has been around for centuries, commonly attributed to the English philosopher Jeremy Bentham. Bentham's theory is rooted in the idea that we should pursue whatever brings the greatest happiness to the greatest number of people. Leaders in education are compelled to make decisions annually, monthly, weekly, and daily. It is not humanly possible to make a decision that is going to suit the needs of every student, parent, or staff member. Moreover, a leader is tasked with making decisions that will affect individuals differently. An effective leader will do their best to make decisions that are in alignment with the school's vision and provide the greatest good for the greatest number of people. Of course, there is no one-size-fits-all decision, and the Utilitarian Doctrine is not foolproof. The educational setting will include instances where morality and ethics need to be considered more fully before a decision is made. Leaders should use discernment.

At the end of the day, the decisions made by an administrative leader must support the safety of students and staff and protect the mission and vision of the school. Leaders should never rewrite the rules based on a temporary situation or circumstance, or in response to an exception to the rule. Rules like this would only benefit a small number of people. Rules and decisions need to be grounded in rational thinking. Reasonable people will understand and support reasonable decisions. A leader's ability to make good decisions will ultimately strengthen the relationships within the educational community.

Relationships

To be effective, leaders must build rapport both within the school setting and with the greater community. Humans are naturally social beings, and relationships are an essential part of the human experience. Because connecting with others is a human need, positive relationships serve as the foundation for the type of community-building and culture that are conducive to creating great schools. Every educational leader at every position needs to be in tune with how human nature and personal experience impact relationship-building. There are commonalities among humans; how one thinks, feels, and behaves is largely determined by one's life experiences. When dealing with colleagues, parents, students, and other educational constituents, a leader has to work to understand different perspectives, then look for opportunities to connect and build shared experiences. These positive relationships will serve as a cornerstone to student achievement.

Internal Communication

As leaders communicate with one another, parents, and students, it increases the possibility of building positive relationships and maximizing student learning. Like all good relationships, communication is the key to its success. In education, communication is essential to the school's success.

Structured, efficient internal communication at a school site is essential to daily operations. It shapes the rhythm and flow of the operations, creating connection among the employees and minimizing confusion and frustration. Lack of information leaves staff feeling as though they are not a part of the process. Effective communication establishes transparency and builds trust. Staff members will feel more comfortable serving as advocates for the school when they are well-informed. Strong internal communication can improve safety measures and create a shared understanding of new efforts and improvements throughout the year. The role communication plays in the implementation of practices and procedures that contribute to the mission and vision of the school cannot be understated.

Characteristics of an Effective Leader

- Courageous
- Positive
- Relationship-builder
- Compassionate
- Role model
- Cultivates leadership in others
- Hard worker
- Holds high standards
- Likeable
- Always learning and growing
- Problem-solver
- Resilient
- Transparent
- Optimistic

Leaders use these skills and characteristics to manage the demands, responsibilities, and pressures that they are uniquely equipped to handle on a daily basis. This requires mental and emotional stability and strength. The demands and complexities of leadership can be taxing, and there has to be a way to mitigate burnout and stress.

Self-Care

People who have a calling on their lives are by default purpose-driven, but their dedication to that calling is both exhilarating and exhausting. The adrenaline and drive take a mental,
emotional, and even a physical toll. The stress and pressure of
leadership in education runs far and wide. Education is a delicate
profession because leaders are charged with transforming the
minds and lives of students. The world is counting on educators
to produce students who are going to contribute to the world in
a positive way.

In order to be the best for others, educators have to take care
of themselves. It is like when flight attendants tell adults to first
put on their own oxygen mask in an emergency before taking care
of their children. Self-care is critical to maximizing an educator's
effectiveness, and it starts with creating and maintaining *balance*.
Without self-care, burnout can be the result. Any amount of effort
or energy given to the job cannot overcome the gap that is created
when teachers and staff are emotionally burned out, physically
ill, or physically and emotionally drained. The mental health and
well-being of leaders requires educators to manage and balance the
emotional journey of life.

Balance is created through strategies and routines used as pre-
ventative measures to minimize mental and emotional fatigue and
to manage stressors, both the by-products of the profession and in
one's personal life. Time invested in self-care helps educators stay
fueled, positive, and mentally healthy. Self-care also helps create
much-needed space between an educator's personal life and professional life. In the same way that separation between the logs in a fire
allows for a better flame, the separation between work and home
keeps the fire burning for the profession. A commitment to self-care
not only sets up positive mental health, but it can also become a
meaningful outlet for personal growth and relationship-building,
as seen in these strategies:

- Regular exercise: 30 minutes, 5 days a week
- Healthy eating
- Quality sleep (8 hours is ideal)
- Daily meditation and/or mindfulness
- Read and/or listen positive messages daily (books, podcasts, etc.)
- Surround yourself with positive people
- Practice gratitude (perhaps by journaling)
- Cultivate hobbies
- Find ways to serve
- Live life through love

Living life through love is liberating, and it releases stressors caused by anger, resentment, hate, etc. A life lived through love provides that much-needed exhale that creates calmness and peace.

Conclusion

It is impossible to create and maintain great schools without effective educational leadership. Each member of the leadership team at a school site must understand and own their role as a leader. Administrative leaders need to be attuned to employee personalities and intentionally interact and engage with staff according to their individual employee personality. Knowing how to connect with a wide array of personalities distinguishes effective leaders from ineffective leaders. Good educational leaders intuitively go about building positive relationships with colleagues, parents, students, and other stakeholders.

Every staff member is a part of the educational leadership team, and the school's success requires that they take ownership of their specific role in day-to-day operations and interactions with students, parents, and other employees. Leaders accept responsibility for making decisions that impact stakeholders and recognize that it is impossible to please everyone. By applying the Utilitarian Doctrine, leaders can approach decisions with a goal of providing the greatest good for the greatest number of people. Good decision-making and effective communication will create a foundation for positive relationships and better schools. Furthermore, school leaders must be intentional about using internal communications at the school site to achieve a connected community. The stress that results from the demands of educational leadership requires educators to create balance in their daily lives so that they can endure the pressures of the position and hold on to their passion for the work.

CHAPTER SUMMARY

- Administrative leaders have to navigate different layers of people, personalities, and processes to be successful in their jobs.

- Administrative leaders must connect with employees based on their Individual Employee Personality (IEP).

- Effective leadership entails building relationships. Building rapport with everyone in the school ecosystem and the greater community is an important part of building a successful school.

- School administrators need to acknowledge everyone who works at a school site as part of the leadership team.

- Every employee, regardless of their title, is a leader.

- Regardless of how great a school's program may be, there will always be someone who has a complaint.

- Effective leaders do their best to make decisions that align with the greatest good for the greatest number of people.

- Self-care is critical to maximizing one's effectiveness as an educator and maintaining mental health.

- It's essential for leaders (and all educators) to create adequate space between their personal and professional lives to fuel their passion for the profession.

CHAPTER 4

The Business of Education

Serving the Customer Well

*"Far and away the best prize that life has to offer is the chance
to work hard at work worth doing."*

—THEODORE ROOSEVELT, *26th U.S. president*

Schools are businesses that are designed to provide a service. Like other businesses that provide a service, education offers an intangible but extremely high-value product. Schools should provide students with a quality education in a safe and nurturing environment. In order to do so, there has to be a meaningful focus on the school's vision, which will inform all business decisions that are made that contribute to the delivery of the fundamental services. Quality educational services translate to good customer service and excellent academic output. The ultimate goal of the educational business is for leaders to render exceptional service to the parents, students, community partners, and ultimately, to society and the world.

First-Rate Customer Service

In education, it can be easy to overlook the concept of providing professional, high-quality customer service because the service is provided for free in most cases. Free goods and services are typically valued lower than those offered at a cost. When people pay for a good or service, they have higher expectations for the return on their investment. The bigger the investment, the higher the expectation on the return.

Businesses that sell a product or service use quality as a competitive edge to differentiate them from their rivals. Education needs to conduct its business as a five-star industry, taking into consideration the many aspects of customer service that are needed to deliver a quality educational experience. Excellent customer service must be intentional when interacting with customers (parents, students, and associates) in person, on the phone, by email, in letters sent home, on social media, etc. There should always be attention given to ideas that will deliver a high level of service. This investment will create loyal customers who are eager to spread the word about the school and refer other like-minded families. The experience that parents, students, and other partners have when visiting the school and interacting with staff should communicate what is unique about the school and leave a lasting impression. Schools need to develop a mindset of excellence to elevate the public's perception and establish education as a premier industry.

The front office is the first line of contact with families and anyone who visits the school. The standard for the experience that an individual will have at the school is set by the office staff, so this first encounter must be positive. People who come to the school should feel welcomed from the moment that they enter. A simple greeting and a genuine smile is the "first line of excellence" in customer service. The front office will convey the energy and feel of the school and set the expectation of the campus experience for visitors. To provide excellent customer service, the office, the first line of excellence, has to deliver. Once visitors move past the front office, the bar has been set high, and the next interaction has to maintain that same high level of service. If the visitor has a poor initial exchange, the next employee they encounter will need to work that much harder to erase any negative thoughts or sentiments. To be successful, schools need to operate like a business that is focused on delivering excellent customer service.

How to Deliver Excellent Customer Service

Build rapport with the customer: Building positive relationships with parents and students helps to achieve the school's mission and vision. Good relationships make both parents and students feel welcome at school. Face-to-face encounters that include a friendly smile and a genuine greeting can go a long way in strengthening the relationship. Being intentional about greeting individuals by name also adds a personal touch. When taking phone calls, this can be accomplished by answering with a smile. Positive intonation and energy resonate even on the phone and make the caller feel welcome.

Always listen to the customer: People just want to be heard. Always listen to the customer. In many cases they just want their feelings to be acknowledged. Once they have said what they need to say, their feelings should be validated—even just by saying, "I'm sorry you feel that way." If the problem can be corrected, it should be done. If it cannot be remedied as requested, offer another solution, and explain why it can't be resolved in the manner they would like. Do not respond by saying, "These are the rules," even if that is, in fact, true. Do explain why specific rules or policies exist. An example would be a student who was asked to walk and not run in the hallway. When asking that student to walk, a follow-up response would be to explain it as a safety issue. "We want to keep you and others safe, and that is why we do not want students running in the hallway."

Show empathy to the customer: Empathizing with the client helps to create or strengthen the bond. When an educator is able to see things from the client's perspective, it allows them to bring more grace to any given situation. Parents are passionate about their children, and they can get emotional at times. An educational leader needs to put themselves in the client's position and under-stand how they may feel. If, for example, a parent feels as though their child is being bullied, and they are upset about an incident, it helps to imagine *being the parent* who feels that their child is being bullied at school, and then assist in a way that might be of support to them. With that in mind, the educational leader would first ask themself, "How would I want to be supported in this situation if I were in their shoes?" Empathizing with students is also important. In the case of elementary and even middle schools, remember that these students will see things from a child's perspective. The educational staff must recognize the child's point of view and tailor their approach and interaction accordingly.

Respond as soon as possible: The home-school connection is a huge part of a student's success. Oftentimes administrators, teachers, and support staff are not available to others during the school hours, particularly if they are supervising students. When dealing with parents or other business-related individuals, responding to communications received via email, phone, or by letter as soon as possible is critical to providing superior service. Responding promptly to someone's question or addressing their concerns lets them know that they are valued. When a parent has a concern, an immediate response reduces their frustration and is more likely to restore them to a feeling of satisfaction. Community and business leaders are also customers or associates of the school. Engaging with the community in a way that builds rapport is the ultimate goal. Timely responses to the requests and demands of businesses and community partners will enhance the relationships.

Be a problem solver: Customers will approach school leaders to address any issues that come up. They will address any member of the team that they feel is associated with the problem or anyone who they feel can help them. School leaders should always hear what the customer has to say and seek a solution to the problem. When addressing any problem, it is best to attempt to provide a solution that is pleasing to the customer. If it's unclear what would be the best solution for the customer, it is a best practice to ask, "What can I do to help make the situation better for you?" In order to provide excellent customer service, problem-solving is a must. There are simple processes that educational leaders can follow to address problems, but the first step is to *listen*. Be clear about the nature of the problem. Gain an understanding as to what solution would satisfy the client. Weigh any and all solutions that are going to make the customer happy. Decide on a solution that is both beneficial to the customer and the operation of the business.

Know the customer: Students, parents, and community members are repeat customers. Getting to know them is key to building positive relationships and working cohesively together to support the vision of the school. When teachers know their students, that connection motivates students to engage in class and maximize learning. There are many benefits to getting to know parents, as they can and should be used as allies in their child's education. Getting to know parents involves customizing the interaction to meet their personality style. If a parent is more traditional, it might be important to address them as Mr. or Mrs. Smith. On the other hand, a parent might prefer to be less formal and feel more comfortable being called by their first name. With parents who have a sense of humor, jokes here and there are welcome. Other parents may have a more serious demeanor. Get to know each parent and try to meet them on their individual level. It establishes mutual respect and creates a positive relationship.

Correct your mistakes: Everyone is human. We all make mistakes. When this happens, acknowledge the mistake, and do what is necessary to correct it. Being dishonest or trying to cover up a mistake will only compound the problem. It will leave the impression that the client is being deceived, and it will be difficult to have trust going forward. Owning up to a mistake is an opportunity to connect on a human level and demonstrate the qualities of authenticity and honesty. It will also increase the likelihood of the customer responding with grace. This shows integrity, which often earns the customer's respect. In the future, they will be less likely to question the validity of what they are being told or specific actions taken. They know from experience that they are dealing with individuals who have integrity. When a mistake is corrected, it is important to make the client relationship whole again. If there was an error in a grade given on a child's report card, ensure that the grade is corrected, and provide the parents with the updated report card. If a child missed out on an opportunity because of an error, provide the child with another opportunity of equal or higher value. Correct mistakes expeditiously and accompany the remedy with an apology. Being apologetic shows sincerity.

Go the extra mile: Go above and beyond to make the customer feel good about their experience at the school. When you are charged with a task, meet the expectation, and then go the extra mile. This is a mindset that reflects a spirit of excellence—and is always found in the details. It could be a simple gesture that enhances the experience and leaves a lasting impression. When schools go the extra mile, they add value to the services they provide and create a culture of providing excellent service to stakeholders. This could be a simple act of acknowledging someone in the hallway or a more coordinated plan to support a family in need.

Get feedback: To provide excellent service, schools can gather feedback to assess their efforts. Constructive criticism will identify areas of strength and opportunities for improvement in the program. An annual survey is an effective way to get data on the school's performance across different areas such as academics, teachers, administration, safety, and overall service. On the survey, there should be a section where parents and students can write in comments to address any additional topics. Simply having an accessible suggestion box in the main office or a common area is another way to get ongoing feedback. Lastly, the Parent Teacher Association (PTA) is an avenue through which schools can receive positive, scheduled feedback. Committing to multiple evaluation tools is an essential part of providing excellent customer service.

Think long-term: The reputation a school creates for itself based on high-quality customer service will have a lasting impact and effect for years to come. Long after the customer has a child at the school, they will continue to talk about the school in a positive light and will continue to refer individuals to the school. When people feel good about a service that is provided, their testimonials make for good marketing. Thinking about the long-term success of the school leads to vitality.

Marketing

Marketing is another aspect of school business. After all, student enrollment is one of the primary sources of revenue for public, private, and parochial schools. Maximizing enrollment is necessary to provide the revenues needed to fund the daily operations of the school. A school that is providing a quality education should want to maximize enrollment in order to educate as many students as possible. There are a variety of ways to market the school, i.e. fliers, postcards, newspaper ads, community events, etc., however the marketing messaging needs to convey the mission and vision of the school. Leadership should work together to identify the best strategy, whether that be to highlight key features of school success, enrichment programs, or high-test scores. Current customers can be used for marketing. Testimonials from parents and students add a personal touch. Again, the best marketing is free—excellent service will compel customers and business partners to spread the word about the school.

Facility Operations and Maintenance

The foundation of the day-to-day operations of the school business cannot overlook facilities and maintenance. A variety of services need to be performed to ensure that the facility is in proper working order to deliver the intended business services to its customers. In the business of schools, the facility itself is integral to carrying out the business of educating students. The facility must be in good condition, and focus must be on ensuring that day-to-day operations run smoothly and at their maximum capability.

Safety is the first point of interest. Maintenance of the school facility increases the likelihood of safety and functionality. The regulation of classroom temperature, both the heating and air conditioning, fall under facility operation and maintenance. Also included is the maintenance of the grounds—gardening, irrigation systems, water and power, weather mitigation, trash, custodial duties, internet service, etc. The repairs and other regular services involved with facility operations and maintenance are not sexy, but they are extremely important to the daily operations of school business.

Finances

Understanding the ins and outs of finance is vital to successfully running a school. In general, public-school funding includes a combination of federal, state, and local funding, but the bulk of it comes from the state. Property and state taxes provide a large portion of local and state funding, which can be problematic for a variety of reasons, one being that more affluent areas will receive more funding if other systems are not in place to level the funding distribution. Another involves public interest and how they choose to support schools financially with tax increases, bond measures, etc. Ultimately, the goal of state funding models is to distribute funding equitably to schools. Local funding is generated from property taxes. Federal funding reflects roughly 10 percent of a school's budget. Private and parochial schools rely on tuition, grants from charitable organizations, and private donors.

Revenues are necessary to sustain the school business. Per pupil spending, cash flow, and accounting are additional facets of school finance that dictate how the budget balances. Budgeting and budget projections support fiscal planning. Knowledge of the monthly and annual revenues help maintain a budget that creates solvency. Fiscal management is key to current and future success, and fiscal responsibility is essential to educational vitality. Depending on the school model (public, private, parochial), funding analysis and revenue streams will dictate the school's ability to cover its operating costs and fund programs.

Other Funding

Fundraising, grants, and individual donors make up the other sources of revenue that schools receive. Fundraising is a common way for schools to offset expenses or to pay for specific projects. Families of the school often work to raise money through fundraising activities. The type of fundraising activity and the number of families participating will determine if the fundraiser is a success. Fundraisers should consider both the earning power and the effort it takes to carry out the fundraiser. If the effort required outweighs the earning potential, the fundraiser is probably not worth doing.

Local, state, and federal grants are another common way for schools to obtain money to fund specific projects, to pay for resources, or to offset overhead expenses. School grants range from a few hundred dollars to millions, and the application process can be extremely competitive.

For nonprofit organizations, individual or private donors make up the largest source of charitable donations, roughly 70 percent. Donations can be one-time or recurring streams of income. The potential to raise more than half of a school's fundraising goal from individual donors is high, so it makes sense for schools to put a considerable amount of energy and effort into soliciting private donors.

Human Resources

Education is a matter of the heart. Employing individuals who have a heart and passion for children and education is serious business when designing great schools. Human resources management and leadership is a central part of an educational organization. The roles and responsibilities of the human resources department are numerous and varied. This department builds the framework for the organization, as it supports the hiring, retaining, and firing of employees. School systems handle human resources in a variety of ways. In public schools, the human resources department is generally handled at the district level. Charter, private, and parochial schools typically handle human resources at the site level. In any case, human resources shares the same function in its focus to achieve the mission and vision of a school.

Human Resources Management

- Recruiting and retaining the right people for the right jobs
- Health and safety of staff
- Maintaining a safe environment
- Compensation and employee benefits including health, medical, and life insurance
- 401(k) plans
- Risk management
- Employee and labor relations
- Employer-employee relations
- Labor law compliance
- Payroll taxes
- Sick time and vacation time
- Employee records and files
- Promotion, separation, grievances, welfare administration, job evaluation, and exit interview

The human resources department must also adapt and evolve with the school. In education, the interviewing and hiring process needs to take place at the school site. To hire the right individuals for the school mission and vision, and to create and preserve the culture of the school, it is imperative that the school leaders are charged with the interviewing process.

Human resources is also key to creating and maintaining a positive culture and school environment, which are important for retaining employees and supporting their mental health. The human resources department also serves as a check and balance for school leaders.

Governing Board

Educational institutions that are nonprofit organizations are governed by a board. The members of the governing board are public officials. The professional and ethical shared responsibility of the board is to ensure that *all students* are served with equity and receive a high-quality education in a safe environment. The governing board is a decision-making body for a school district or a school that provides oversight and accountability, establishes policies, and maintains fiscal responsibility in alignment with the mission and vision of the district or school. Board decisions should focus on distributing resources equitability and ensuring access for all students in the district schools and the community.

The governing board members serve the community in which they reside, and their role is to have a powerful impact on students enrolled in their local schools. Each governing board member is bound by their belief and commitment to the mission and vision of the school district. The district's mission and vision should be streamlined with the mission and vision of individual schools in the district. The governing board should know and understand the district's goals and how the goals of each individual school tie into and apply to the district's goals. The governing board must ensure that district goals contribute to the mission and vision of the individual schools. As the educational industry moves toward creating vitality in schools, it is important to build strong and effective governing boards. These are the hub of every school district or school. They set the tone for the direction and effectiveness of the school district at-large and, ultimately, for every school within the district.

The traditional governing board limits its duties and responsibilities to making decisions at the monthly board meetings. The traditional board model must evolve to take on a more progressive and expansive role in schools. The new board model will need bold and courageous board members who will challenge their leaders, systems, and practices. They will need to take an active approach to governing by connecting with stakeholders at the school site and ensuring that the decisions made are reflective of not only the district's mission and vision, but also that of the individual school sites, and, most importantly, students—*all students.* These board members must be committed to actively learning how they can support each school site.

Board members must be one with the people—not just certain people, but all people. Getting up close and personal with the school's administrators, staff, students, and parents is necessary to gain an insight, perspective, and understanding of what is happening, how people are feeling, and how they can be of service in supporting the school's goals. The closer public officials get to the people they serve, the more effective they can be as members of the governing board.

The governing of schools is a huge responsibility, and elected officials take on an ethical oath to represent all students and ensure that there is equity and access. Equity and access in schools will help our country move toward reversing the historical injustices imposed on people of color-thus dismantling racism in education. Exclusion and disadvantage have been the narrative for people of color in America. Now, more than ever, equity, and access must be a priority for the governing board. It should be a part of every conversation and all of the decisions being made. There should be district-wide guidelines delineating how each school is providing resources and ensuring that policies and procedures are geared toward leveling the playing field for the oppressed and disadvantaged. The work that needs to occur requires ongoing assessments of the practices at each site that contribute to inclusion, equity, and access.

The governing board sets the tone for the culture of the school district and should consider the culture and climate that it wants to resonate in its schools and in the community. The attitudes and beliefs of the governing board speak to the parents and community at-large, thereby reflecting the attitudes and beliefs of the district, and ultimately communicates the district's educational philosophy and how diverse groups of children will be treated.

Conclusion

Education is a business. In this context, providing excellent customer service boils down to making sure that the customer is pleased with the service being provided. Every aspect of a school's operations ties directly or indirectly to the goal of providing a quality education to students. With that in mind, the caliber of functioning in the different areas of operation will dictate the level of customer service provided. The business operation of a school includes professional, ethical, fiscal, and legal responsibilities. Business culture weighs heavily on the quality of service provided. A business-minded school culture reflects the norms, values, rituals, traditions, and beliefs of the district, schools, and their employees. The business culture has an impact on strategic planning. It influences management and the decisions they make. In order for education to become a respected industry, districts and schools must elevate their business model to reflect premier service. To create great schools, it is imperative to build effective, well-intentioned governing boards. Every child deserves to attend a great school that serves all students with equity and excellence. When the service provided is a child's education and future, the service must be excellent.

CHAPTER SUMMARY

- Schools are businesses that are designed to provide a service. Like other businesses that provide a service, education offers an intangible product that is of extreme value.

- The ultimate goal of the educational business is for leaders to render exceptional service to the parents, students, and any community partners.

- In education, it can be easy to overlook the importance of customer service because the service provided is free in most cases.

- There must be intention when interacting with parents, students, and associates, whether in person, on the phone, by email, in letters sent home, on social media, etc.

- The front office is the first line of contact with families and visitors to the school. The office staff sets the standard for the experience.

- To deliver excellent customer service, build rapport with the customer, always listen to the customer, show empathy, respond as soon as possible, problem-solve, get to know the customer, correct your mistakes, go the extra mile, think long-term, and get feedback.

- School funding includes a combination of federal, state, and local funding. The goal of state funding models is to distribute funding equitably to schools.

- Private and parochial schools rely on tuition, grants from charitable organizations, and private donors.

- Consider human resources as a critical resource in the effort to build a school focused on achieving its mission and vision.

- The governing board is a decision-making body for a school district or a school that establishes policies and provides oversight, accountability, and fiscal responsibility in alignment with the mission and vision of the district and schools.

- When the product is as important as a child's education, the service must be top-notch.

- Schools have to develop a mindset of excellence and quality in order for the overall vibe of education in this country to elevate to a premier industry.

PART 2

PARTNERSHIP

Strength of the Child

CHAPTER 5

Parents

A Child's First Teachers

*"At the end of the day, the most overwhelming key
to a child's success is the positive involvement of parents."*

—JANE D. HULL, *American politician and educator*

Today, many children have unconventional home dynamics. Guardians and caregivers can include adoptive and foster parents, grandparents, or other well-meaning adults who take on the role of parent. There are countless scenarios of living angels who assume the role and responsibility of being a parent-like figure to a child. For that reason, anyone who provides for a child's needs, above and beyond food and shelter, will be referred to as a parent.

A multitude of research has been done on the impact that parent engagement and involvement has on a child's education. The research shows that positive parent involvement helps to maximize student achievement. The more a parent is involved at school, the better the quality of the education a student receives. There is an old adage that compares education to a three-legged stool, supported equally by the commitment of the educator, student, and parent. If one or more of the parties is not invested in the process, the student will struggle. Schools are always searching for ways to educate parents on how to support their child and get involved with their child's education and the school. When parents are actively engaged in the school, it benefits both the student and school, and it communicates to the student that education is a priority. At the end of the day, parents are partners with teachers in their child's education. The more parents engage with the school, working toward the school's mission and vision, the better the school.

Parents are a child's first teachers. From the time a child comes out of the womb, they are predisposed to learning. In these early stages, it is the parent's obligation to foster a love of learning and reading in their child. Parents are responsible for teaching their children early literacy skills and primary academic instruction, such as ABCs, 123s, colors, shapes, animals, etc. Reading to a child daily is critical to developing their early literacy skills and nurturing a love of learning. Parents are charged with the responsibility of instructing their infants and toddlers in preparation for entry into school and the world.

Social behavior is first learned in the home as a natural part of the parent-child interaction. Children inherently begin their lessons on social behavior through their observations of parents, siblings, and other individuals who live in and visit the home. This includes learning manners and knowing when to say "please" and "thank you." Emotional behaviors are also intuitively learned in the home environment. This is where children learn when to be happy, mad, sad, and express other emotions.

There is another component of early learning that is often overlooked. How a parent communicates with a child can teach them to become a critical thinker—while with less formal instruction, it must be intentional. When adults consistently have conversations with their child that elicit thought, a child's critical-thinking skills are developed. If that communicative interaction doesn't occur early on, a child's critical-thinking skills can be impaired. Many parents are unaware of the extent to which this impacts how a child receives what is being taught in school. Communication with a toddler involves listening and speaking. When a child is in daily communication with an adult from the time they enter the world, their listening and speaking skills are stronger. Children who enter school with strong listening and speaking skills are in a position to be successful academically.

Parents must be intentional about how they raise their children, even before the child is born. Planning for the future involves parents envisioning where they would like to see their child long-term, including what skills, values, and ethics they want their child to have and how they want their child to interact with the world around them. A child's behavior, along with their ability to think and listen critically, and work cooperatively in a group setting should be taken into consideration when parents are setting goals for their children.

A parent is also charged with instilling the importance of education in their child. This is accomplished through a parent's actions, engagement, and involvement in their child's education. Most parents will not say that education is unimportant, but their actions may communicate that other things are valued more than school and learning. Children follow the lead of their parents. They learn to value what their parents value, adopting the same mindset. Raising children is an investment, and parents have to be willing to invest their *time* in order to get a big return.

The educational community has witnessed parents whose actions demonstrate that education is not important to them. These parents are completely disengaged with the educational process. They do not check their child's homework, they do not attend back-to-school nights or parent teacher conferences, etc. They have no idea what is going on at school. Children pick up on this and respond accordingly. Or maybe there are parents who allow sports to take precedence over education. These parents sit for hours at practice and attend every game, but they never attend school meetings. The children intuitively know that their parents value sports more than education. They will excel in sports because of the priority placed on it, which oftentimes minimizes their academic success. In this instance and others like it, a shift in a parent's priorities is needed to reverse the effects—making sports secondary to academic excellence.

There are other instances where parents are not engaged with their child's education because they are in survival mode and are not mentally or emotionally able to give effort to their child's education or academic success. There are psychological components of development that must be considered. An awareness of the impact of these psychological and social-emotional levels help to guide interaction with parents and form positive relationships with both them and their children. No matter who you are or what type of relationship you are cultivating, the bottom line is that everyone wants to be heard and know that what they have to say and how they feel matters. Everyone needs compassion and grace. Unless it has been communicated by the student or parent, there is no way to know what is happening in someone's life, what they are experiencing emotionally, mentally, or psychologically.

Maslow's Hierarchy of Needs

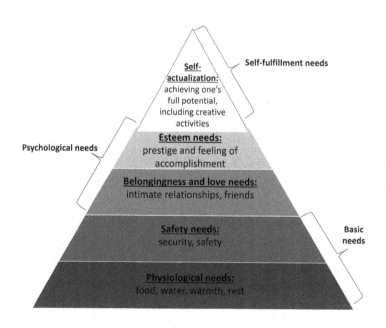

Interacting with Students and Parents

Abraham Maslow proposed "A Theory of Human Nature" that looks at the processes of human development through a hierarchy of psychological needs and wants. Maslow suggests that humans operate from three primary needs: basic needs, psychological needs, and self-fulfillment needs. Maslow created a diagram to depict five distinct levels of need. The lower levels of the pyramid reflect the most basic physiological and safety needs. The intermediate levels include psychological needs—the need to feel a sense of belonging and love from others and a personal sense of accomplishment. From there, the highest need of self-fulfillment, or achieving one's full potential, can begin. Maslow noted that it is possible to move on to a higher level even if a lower level has not been fully met; however, the primary and secondary needs cannot go unaddressed if an individual aspires to achieve self-actualization.

In navigating relationships with parents, educators can use this understanding to accommodate individual personalities and different levels of engagement and interaction. Parents operate from their own psychological level of needs when they enter the educational arena. Maslow's hierarchy of needs can provide educators with insight on parental behavior, decision-making, and the extent of their engagement in their child's education. There are many adults who are operating from basic needs. According to Maslow's pyramid, basic needs include the lowest two levels of needs. The lowest need is physiological: food, water, warmth, and rest. The next level of basic need includes security and safety. It is important for people to have these basic needs before they fully engage with their psychological needs. The psychological needs, as depicted in the diagram, include a sense of belonging, feeling loved, and esteem needs. Belonging and love are found in intimate relationships and friendships. Esteem needs include a personal feeling of accomplishment or importance. The final level of needs is self-actualization. Individuals arrive at this level when they feel as though they have reached their full potential. Personal growth is essential for self-actualization.

It is important for parents and educators to understand that this process of human behavior is motivated by an individual's present and future wants and needs. Educators should take into consideration where a parent may be on Maslow's hierarchy of needs because where they are positioned will dictate how they engage in their child's education. It can explain their educational motivation, their priorities, and the strength of their engagement and involvement.

When a parent is struggling and in survival mode, their child's education will likely take a back seat as they try to meet their family's basic needs. Parents who are able to have more of their mental and psychological needs met will have a greater capacity to engage in the educational process with their child. Maslow's hierarchy of needs does not explain the full complexity of the behaviors, motivation, and engagement of parents; there are other factors to consider. However, this basis for understanding human nature can promote empathy toward parents and students.

Parent Personalities

It is so important for educators to understand that they are going to encounter a myriad of parent personalities. These personalities have been developed and defined by a family's history, experiences, trauma, and current circumstances. How parents raise their children is a direct reflection of their own childhood experiences, good and bad, and these will show up in their child's education. In order to be effective in any capacity or position, educators must learn to navigate difficult personalities because parents are an invaluable part of the educational process. Understanding the range of parent personalities can assist educators in managing the relationships and engaging parents in the most effective way. Every parent is different; however, there are seven dominant characteristics that describe how many parents approach the educational experience. Parents can be found on the spectrum of the following personality categories, or they may toggle between one or more types during the course of a year or over several years.

The Samurai

The Samurai parent is the ideal parent in an educational setting. Educators love the Samurai because they are the parents who are engaged, supportive, and cooperative. They look for ways to volunteer and support the teachers and the school. They keep abreast of all the things going on at school by reading information sent home, and they participate in fundraisers. Samurai parents place a high value on education, and they make it a priority. More importantly, the children of Samurai parents are, like most students, a reflection of their parents. These students are well-behaved and perform well academically. The children of the Samurai parents understand the importance of education and enjoy learning. These parents are actively engaged with the school, and it is important that they be recognized and appreciated for their work and dedication.

The Berserk

Every educator has experienced the disruptive and destructive nature of the Berserk parent. They can be passive, active, or aggressive. In any form, their behavior is an annoyance for educators, and it can even impede the educational process for their child and the school at times. When the Berserk parent is provoked, all hell breaks loose. The Berserk parent is not rational and often speaks nonsensically. This parent does not necessarily know that their behavior is disrespectful, inappropriate, or difficult. The Berserk parent can be loud and boisterous or emotional and quiet. It is not uncommon for this type of parent to become emotionally vulnerable. It is imperative to remember that when someone is emotionally charged, they do not have the ability to think rationally. They are fueled by their emotions, and critical thinking goes out the window. It is difficult to have a conversation with this type of parent when they are agitated.

It has been my experience that many Berserk parents have a lot of time on their hands. It might be a coincidence, but the saying "an idle mind is a playground for the Devil" also rings true. Without anything productive to occupy their time, Berserk parents often seek out mischief and destruction. Many people have a history of some sort of childhood trauma that manifests in their lives as adults, so educators need to remember that any outbreaks or disruptions by these parents are not personal.

When encountering a Berserk parent, it is best to listen and hear them out. Oftentimes when someone is upset, they just want to be heard. Assessing the situation and determining the direction the parent is going will dictate how to best respond. If the parent is verbally abusive or even becoming aggressive or threatening, educators should remove themselves from the situation. Reacting to someone who is irate will only compound the problem. In difficult situations, it is best to respond, not react. A reaction is impulsive and unprofessional—similar to the behavior of the parent. Stooping to their level will not resolve the situation. The goal is always to be a problem-solver. Working to de-escalate the situation and address the problem is always the best strategy. A professional, calm response creates an opportunity to remedy the situation.

The Traitor

There are parents who show up well-intentioned, supportive, and helpful—until something triggers a shift. It could be something that they are struggling with in their personal life or something that does not go their way. Whether it is as simple as a school decision that they don't agree with or an unfavorable incident involving their child, they become public enemy number one. They go from being a supportive parent to becoming adversarial or disruptive—like a traitor. This unpredictability can be ongoing, as the Traitor swings back and forth with their mood, and it may become difficult to know their frame of mind. Traitors force educators to walk on eggshells. Being in tune with the Traitor's triggers and learning how to communicate with them based on their personality will help minimize any conflicts that might occur.

The Impostor

Social media has had a profound impact on both children and adults. Social media has created a false reality for those who actively engage with it, as it gives individuals an opportunity to create their ideal self. Portraying the ideal self for friends and the audience-at-large online can become an addiction, and, unfortunately, the real self then takes a back seat. Eventually, the ideal self-morphs into the real self in the mind of the Impostor, and the ideal self becomes a persona that is represented in real life.

Impostor parents want to paint a picture-perfect life, like a social media junkie. These parents don't want to admit to any deficiencies in their involvement with their child's education. Impostor parents want to be seen as Samurai parents. They know the role that they should play in their child's life, and they maintain that facade for as long as they can through misleading statements and avoidance. Unfortunately, something will inevitably challenge that facade and shine a light on the true Impostor parent, their character, and values. The Impostor will either become upset or they will avoid the situation when they are confronted with the truth. A gentle, honest approach is necessary with this parent. Share observations related to the child's performance and offer recommendations. Ultimately, it is up to the Impostor to decide if they can be genuine and address any concerns for the sake of their child.

The Ghost

As the name implies, these parents are like ghosts, and the teacher is lucky to see them at any given time during the school year. The Ghost parent typically has someone drop their kid off at school in the morning, and someone else picks them up after school. On the rare occasion when they do appear, they are in a rush and avoid conversations about their child. Children of Ghost parents typically struggle academically. They do not complete homework assignments and are often unprepared for tests. Projects that are required to be done at home are usually not completed. Oftentimes Ghost parents will show up to complain or make an accusation that their child is being mistreated. The Ghost parent who shows up to support their child's poor behavior or inaccurate accusations does so as a way to show the child they care about them. Parents who are not actively engaged in their child's life find other ways to show their child that they care about them. It could be by buying them things, defending them, or supporting unacceptable behavior. These parents will also appear if their child is in a school performance. Learning some of the challenges that prevent the Ghost parent from engaging in their child's education can help educators find creative ways to include them in the educational process.

The Bandwagoner

Like children, there are parents who are subject to peer pressure, looking to fit in or join in on the drama. These parents do not have healthy social lives, and they look to their child's school as their own social outlet. They attach themselves to the parents of their child's friends. They seek to align with other individuals who are disruptive to the educational process. There are both extreme and mild cases, but be aware of how Bandwagoner parents can hinder the progress of the school's vision. When this happens, it should be nipped in the bud before it gets out of hand. Identify the source of the drama and address whatever issue people are rallying around. Do not allow Bandwagoners to turn against a specific teacher, administrator, staff member, or the school. Positive parent groups can help dismantle destructive Bandwagoners by using their voice and influence to diffuse the negative works of these types of parents.

The Commoner

Most parents fall into this category. Commoners are those parents who are a presence at the school, and they understand their role as a parent is to send their child to school. Most commoners are relatively cooperative. They are responsive to the rules and requests of the school and the classroom teacher. The children of Commoner parents can be students who excel academically, average students, or those whose academic performance could be low. Commoners are not disruptive. By and large, regardless of how their child is performing, they defer to the educational process, either out of respect or indifference. Commoners can be encouraged to get off the fence and engage a little more with a nudge here and there. Educational leaders should put forth efforts to pull Commoner parents into the realm of Samurai parents.

Education attracts a wide range of personalities. Being aware of what motivates a parent will help to engage them positively and minimize conflict. Educators have to be aware that parents come to education with their own history—and sometimes that history includes unresolved trauma. The childhood experiences of adults, good and bad, will manifest in the rearing of their children. How adults show up at their child's school reflects how they were raised and how they interpret their own childhood experiences. Educators need to engage effectively with all kinds of parents. Responding to different personalities in kind will help educational leaders communicate and interact with parents successfully.

Some parents are open to hearing educational leaders' observations and will support efforts to correct problems in which they or their kids play a role. Defensive parents will have a difficult time taking feedback. They get offended at suggestions and often continue the undesired behavior or even step it up. Ultimately, being cognizant of parent personalities will allow educational leaders to find effective ways to create parent engagement.

Parent Engagement

Parent engagement takes on a deeper level of investment than parent involvement. When a parent is engaged with their child's education, they are hands-on with the child and aligned with teacher expectations and the school's mission and vision. Engaged parents understand the joint responsibility they share with educators and students. When parents are engaged with their child, regardless of the family's income, the student is more likely to achieve academic success. School leaders must put processes and procedures in place at the school site that will support parental engagement and involvement. Communication is a huge component to increasing parental engagement.

Communication

Parents have a responsibility to engage in their child's education, and communication drives that engagement. Parent correspondence with the teacher and the school is important to the child's academic success. Parents who regularly read communication from the teacher and the school know better how to support their child at home. When there is a breakdown in communication, there is a disruption to the education of the child.

The home-school connection is important to parent communication. A bridge to the home is created by communicating with the parent. The home-school connection is a two-way street. When the school reaches out to parents, it is up to parents to be receptive to that communication. When parents communicate with the school, it is important for the school to be responsive to that communication. Parent-initiated communication is an opportunity for educators to build positive relationships with families and maximize a child's learning and social development. Effective partnerships between parents and schools are made possible through consistent and clear communication.

Conclusion

Education is a partnership between parents and the school. Parents are integral to the educational experience. They are the gatekeepers to their child's educational success. The real impact of education is decided by what happens at home, as it will dictate the child's educational belief. Parents are a child's first teachers, and the impact that they have on a child's academic success cannot be overlooked by educators. Parents put on display a wide range of personalities defined by their childhood and life experiences. Their capacity to engage in the educational experience will be affected by the extent to which their own basic, psychological, and self-fulfillment needs have been met. It is important for educational leaders to practice empathy and compassion when interacting with parents, giving them grace when necessary. The key to creating vitality in schools is parent involvement and engagement. The number of partnerships educational leaders build with parents will go a long way to creating a great school. To set students up for success, both school leadership and culture need to communicate the expectation that parents share responsibility in the education of their child.

CHAPTER SUMMARY

- Children are predisposed to learning even as infants.

- Social behavior is learned through a child's observations of parents, siblings, and other individuals in the home. This is also where children learn when to be happy, mad, or sad.

- Parents are responsible for teaching their children early literacy skills.

- When parents consistently have daily conversations with their child that elicit thought, a child's critical-thinking skills are developed.

- Children who enter school with strong listening and speaking skills are in a position to be successful academically.

- Parents have to be intentional in their efforts to raise their children.

- When parents are more involved at school, the child receives a higher quality education.

- Parents communicate that education is a priority through their actions, engagement, and involvement in their child's education. Students usually reflect their parents' views on education and learning.

- Raising children is an investment, and parents have to be willing to invest their time in order to get a big return.

- Education is a partnership between parents and the school. There has to be an expectation set by schools that parents will assume some responsibility in the education of their child.

CHAPTER 6

Students

Investing in a Better Future

*"Treat people as if they were what they ought to be, and you
help them to become what they are capable of becoming."*

—GOETHE, *German poet*

At the core of education are students. When designing educational institutions, everything should be done with the
student in mind because the ultimate goal of schools is for
students to learn. Student learning is influenced by several factors
that extend beyond academic preparation and performance. The
components of education that contribute to human development
address the needs of the whole child and, in turn, strengthen academic success. In order to cultivate the whole child, there needs to
be an intentional effort and focus on all areas of development: intellectual, social, emotional, and self-image. As educators concentrate
on all areas of growth for each student, their ability to maximize
students' learning potential increases exponentially. The overall
maturation of a student's intellectual properties will improve their
potential for long-term success and create options for their future.

Schools draw students from diverse ethnic, cultural, and economic backgrounds. Students come from distinct family backgrounds and a wide range of experiences. Every student is the sum
total of their familiar background, culture, and life experiences that

have shaped their social and emotional identity. Their background and exposure to life contributes to how they behave, receive instruction, and learn at school. As such, educators need to be aware of the complexities that contribute to student personalities.

Self-image plays a key role in how students grow and perform because how students see themselves will dictate what they believe they can accomplish and how they show up in the world. If they believe they are smart, they will have the confidence to excel academically. If children see themselves as important, they will feel a sense of self-worth and overall pride and comfort. The effects of education reach far past the annual experiences of each child during their compulsory education. Providing every child with a fair, equitable, and high-quality education offers a huge benefit—not only to the child, but to society, both economically and socially.

Student Personalities

Classroom dynamics are decided by the mix of students and their personalities. Every student is unique; however, over the years I've noticed that they tend to fall into categories based on the qualities that they display in the classroom setting. These personality types offer insight as to what motivates different behaviors and various levels of performance so teachers can better identify student needs and support student learning.

The Golden Child

The Golden Child is the student that teachers love to have in class. This is the ideal student, both academically and socially. They excel at learning and follow classroom etiquette. This student is eager to learn, participates in class, and follows directions well. The Golden Child is cooperative overall and makes the teacher's job easy. Parental support of the educational process is typically a key factor in the personality of the Golden Child. There is sometimes a risk that this child will not be challenged to reach their full potential. Their cooperative nature can make it easy for educators to miss opportunities to challenge them to reach a higher level. The Golden Child should be provided with ways to grow past their current social and academic status.

The Cruiser

Educators call an average student a Cruiser. These students do the bare minimum, toggling between earning Cs and Ds and occasional Bs. Sometimes the Cruiser appears to be working hard and still manages to make Cs and occasional Bs. It's helpful for this student to be cognizant of their learning style and the study efforts that need to be put forth to achieve higher results. The Cruiser could also be suffering from a social-emotional issue that needs to be addressed. When a student is consistently underperforming, there should be an investigation to identify possible causes so that educators can make adjustments to help maximize the student's academic potential.

The Lethargian

Sometimes mislabeled as "lazy," Lethargian students are simply not motivated to learn. There are myriad reasons for a student's lack of motivation. Poor academic performance can be attributed to a parent's lack of educational priority and, as a result, a child not viewing education as a priority. This student could also be dealing with external or internal issues that consume their social and mental capacity, preventing them from engaging in the academic process. Many of these students are quiet and can be overlooked in the classroom because they are not disruptive. Their grades are not a reflection of their ability because Lethargian students do not apply themselves to learning. A student who falls in this category just needs someone to take an interest in them. The goal is to move the needle with each student. If one teacher can begin the process of nudging the Lethargian student to start engaging in the learning process, the next teacher will be charged with continuing the progress. A consistent effort to build a positive relationship with this student will cultivate their social and emotional development and build momentum for academic achievement.

The Jackhammer

The Jackhammer is a student who consistently creates distractions, either as a class clown or by calling attention to themselves in some other form or fashion. Any student who hinders the educational process in the classroom through unwanted distractions is not usually seeking attention; they are seeking love. This is still the case when they are displaying behaviors that are considered negative. Jackhammer students take away valuable time and instruction from the rest of the students. In most cases, this student is suffering from social-emotional trauma. In order to see positive changes, this social-emotional trauma has to be addressed. The student's parents need to be a part of the conversation and the solution. An effective way to turn this behavior around is to partner with parents to find something that this child is interested in, like art or coding, and incorporate that interest into his or her daily classroom activity.

The Leper

The Leper is socially awkward and has a difficult time navigating social interaction with classmates. Their peers recognize this awkwardness and shy away from interacting with Lepers. Peer interaction is very important for children, and when a student is not accepted by classmates and other students, it disrupts the social experience for this student. Social development is an integral part of education and needs to be supported in conjunction with a student's academic development. In these situations, teachers are charged with the task of facilitating social interaction to support this student in their social development. Anytime a child is not socially maturing at the same rate as their peers, educational leaders need to assess the severity of the delay. If it is determined that the maturation is grossly irregular, steps should be taken to address the issue. Partnering with the parent is critical to support the Leper and their social growth.

The Church Mouse

Predictably quiet and compliant, the Church Mouse student is reluctant to participate in the classroom actively or vocally. Every classroom population includes these students, and they are often overlooked because they do not disrupt the environment. When a child is quiet, it could mean that they are shy, or it could point to a bigger social issue that needs to be addressed. The Church Mouse can be a high-, average-, or low-performing student. The quiet student who is also low performing runs an even bigger risk of falling through the cracks of the educational system. As educators' endeavor to develop the whole child, both the social-emotional and academic growth of these students must be a priority. Once the gravity of any social issues is identified, the issue can be specifically addressed. For example, in the case of a student who is just shy, a teacher could implement a personal goal for the student to raise their hand three times a day and then increase the goal to five times a day. There are simple measures that can be taken to support student growth, and more severe measures may need to be taken if the meekness is due to something other than shyness. Regardless, the situation needs to be assessed and addressed in order to see the student grow and progress socially.

The Potential

> *"There is nothing in a caterpillar*
> *that tells you it's going to be a butterfly."*
>
> —R. BUCKMINSTER FULLER,
> American architect and inventor

All students have the *potential* to be something greater than they are presently. Children are works in progress. They are learning and growing into their purpose in life. Their experiences along their journey are preparing them for their future. Self-image is a huge factor in how students show up in the classroom—and ultimately in the world. As educators encounter a wide range of personalities in the classroom, it is necessary to realize that all students can take who they are today to the next level if they possess a positive self-image. Finding ways to boost a child's self-image could be all it takes for them to maximize their potential.

Every adult in a child's life helps guide and position them for their destiny. Next to parents, teachers are the most influential people in a child's life. What a responsibility! When teachers take an oath to become a teacher, they are making a commitment to play an all-important role in the future success of every child they encounter. Teachers are invaluable, and with the right mindset they can have an even bigger impact on students and, ultimately, on society.

Students should be true to who they are, and adults should encourage them to grow and develop in such a way that their personality becomes an asset and not a liability. This goal requires educators to create a framework for addressing student needs. It is important to remember that student personalities and behaviors are most often a reflection of their home environment, how they are raised, their parents' personalities and priorities, childhood trauma and experiences, or a combination of these life experiences. It's common for a student to fall into more than one personality category, requiring teachers to be even more creative to support that student's learning. While not all student personalities are easy to work with, every student deserves the attention and guidance that will help them transition to the next level and ultimately achieve success.

Investing in a child's self-image can help a child move past any difficulties they are experiencing, both academically or socially, to maximize their potential. If children can begin to see themselves in a different light, it could be a game changer. Educators and parents need to creatively work together to help a child develop a positive self-image. It is important to identify a student's character in order to address how to best serve them in the classroom setting. This is not an attempt to label students, but rather to identify characteristics of each student as a starting point to supporting their needs. From there, teachers and parents can work together to proactively address areas where further development is needed. Knowledge is always power—for teachers, parents, and students.

Students with Special Needs

Students with special needs are an essential part of the student classroom population. These students typically will have an Individualized Education Program (IEP) or a 504 Plan. IEPs and 504 Plans are legal documents fashioned for students who need a specially designed education plan to address their unique and specific educational needs. Special Education programs at each school site are governed and supported by the Individuals with Disabilities Education Act (IDEA), a federal law that makes free and appropriate education available to students with special needs or disabilities.

Special needs can consist of learning differences and disabilities, mental health issues, specific disabilities, and physical or developmental giftedness. Students who have been identified as having special educational needs have an IEP designed to support their specific needs in the least restrictive environment. Individualized Education Programs are developed by a team of educators and parents. Educators should be aware of students in their class with an IEP and adhere to the accommodations and modifications outlined within each student's IEP. Teachers should focus on the goals of students with special needs and use teaching strategies that support each student's learning.

English-Language Learners

English-Language Learners (ELLs) or English Learners (ELs) are terms used in the United States to refer to students in the educational system who are learning English as a second language. A significant portion of the U.S. public educational system is made up of English-Language Learners. In addition to the language barrier, these students are sometimes confronted with additional challenges that inhibit their learning. They often come from lower economic backgrounds, yet another factor that puts them at risk for academic delays.

It is important for educators to know that ELL students learn in the same fashion that native English speakers learn; however, there are specific teaching strategies that can be used to support the educational needs of non-native speakers. As a base, teachers of ELL students should cultivate positive, supporting relationships with students and be culturally responsive. When students feel comfortable with teachers, they are more likely to open up and take chances to speak and participate in class. Taking an interest in the students' native culture and incorporating cultural connection in daily lessons fosters a supportive relationship that embraces the student's identity.

Instructional practices for ELL students should incorporate language skills across all curricular subjects. Language skills include reading, writing, listening, and speaking. The route to learning a second language typically begins with receptive language, listening, and reading. The development of oral and written language follows receptive language. Teachers should be aware that when they see a student responding to oral and written directions, it does not necessarily mean that they have the ability to produce an oral or written response. There should be an emphasis on speaking in order to develop students' productive language skills. By speaking slowly and increasing the wait time for a response, teachers can help ELL students develop the confidence that they need to be successful. Differentiated instruction provides ELL students and English-only students with instructional practices that allow them to learn using a variety of modalities. ELL students also access the curriculum using a variety of modalities (i.e., writing, speaking, drawing, and listening). Scaffolding also provides differentiated instruction so that ELL students are given all the tools necessary to develop fluency. Incorporating the ELL student's native language into lessons simultaneously helps students connect with the lesson and promotes bilingualism.

Student Learning

Critical Thinking

In preparation for the technology and information they will encounter, students need to develop strong critical-thinking skills—the ability to synthesize information to think logically, rationally, and with reason. The processes of critical thinking involve observation, analysis, interpretation, reflection, evaluation, inference, explanation, problem-solving, and decision-making. Standardized tests have been designed to assess the ability to think critically at grade level. In order to adequately prepare students for standardized assessments, and college and career, there has to be more focus on critical thinking.

The skills required are tied to the language skills: reading comprehension, writing, listening, and speaking. The stronger students are in individual language skills, the stronger their critical-thinking skills will be. National standards (or the Common Core State Standards Initiative) were designed to prepare students for college and career. For students to be college- and career-ready, they must be critical thinkers. As educators work toward preparing students for future endeavors, these language skills have to be included in their curriculum planning. Teachers and staff must understand their roles in implementing curriculum and instruction that will strengthen language skills. Each content subject area includes language, so all subject educators need to set an intention to contribute to developing the language skills of their students.

Metacognition

Developing students into strong readers and thinkers should include metacognition, an important skill for a student's learning toolbox. The Merriam-Webster Dictionary defines metacognition as the "awareness or analysis of one's own learning or thinking processes." When students become metacognitive learners, they are independent thinkers and conscientious learners. Metacognition helps students to become resilient when they encounter challenging problems, both academically and socially. The earlier a child starts to develop their metacognitive competencies, the sooner they will develop the reading skills that will allow them to become a critical thinker. Understanding the reading process is a good way to teach metacognition to students.

Reading Comprehension

Reading is the most crucial component to academic success, as it is the foundation for all learning. Reading comprehension is a meaningful way of reading that establishes an understanding of what is being read. It is the ability to recall, infer, and analyze text or content. Students have to be strong readers in order to become critical thinkers. Strong reading comprehension skills will dictate a student's long-term academic success and their ability to become college- and career-ready.

Educators and parents must not discount the processes that contribute to strong reading skills. Phonics, phonology, decoding, fluency, vocabulary, morphology, syntax, and semantics are all important skills needed for reading comprehension development. Students also have to adopt reading practices that allow them to engage with the text. Reading metacognition will set the foundation for expansive metacognitive abilities. Metacognitive reading strategies include making predictions, visualization, making personal connections, monitoring and checking for understanding, and correcting gaps in understanding. Students who use these strategies to engage with the text and sharpen their reading comprehension will have the ability to adapt and use these skills in other areas of their academic learning and personal growth experiences.

Comprehension is vital to all learning and understanding. Showing students how to think about comprehension will translate to metacognition in all areas of their lives, thereby allowing students to become independent learners and take the reins of their future success. Reading provides a foundation for strengthening one's critical thinking and emotional intelligence.

Emotional Quotient

In addition to the language skills, emotional and adaptability quotients should be factored into maximizing a student's critical-thinking skills. An emotional quotient (EQ) is a measure of one's emotional intelligence (EI). Individuals with a high emotional intelligence are in tune with their emotions and can manage them in a way that creates a balance in temperament and mood. Building a high emotional intelligence supports positive mental health. It leads to a high EQ, helping students build healthy peer relationships.

One goal for educational leaders is to assist students in their maturation process, which includes facilitating growth of their EI. A high EI contributes to critical thinking and supports students' overall well-being. Critical thinkers have the ability to think rationally without becoming emotionally charged. It is difficult to think critically while emotions are heightened. As students mature, addressing and developing their emotional intelligence will not only improve their critical-thinking skills, but it will contribute to positive social behavior and interaction. The advanced social skills made prevalent through emotional intelligence reinforces communication skills, conflict resolution, teamwork, empathy, and positive relations. A student's emotional quotient is strengthened by a high adaptability quotient (AQ).

Adaptability Quotient

Intellectual and emotional quotients are widely known and commonly discussed. The adaptability quotient (AQ) is now thought to be valuable, though it had a slow uptake. One's ability to acclimate, adjust, or transform to changing circumstances or a new environment in a healthy manner is known as their adaptability quotient (AQ). Intellectual, emotional, and adaptability quotients are mutually exclusive, but they can complement one another. Change requires people to adapt. Life brings a lot of changes, and the ability to adapt is what separates those who achieve massive success from those who remain stagnant. Students need the skill of adaptation to survive difficult situations, to experience personal growth, and to be marketable in the workforce. Teaching students to cultivate their intellectual, emotional, and adaptability quotients will give them tools to maximize their success.

Mathematics

Mathematical conceptual development also contributes to strengthening a student's critical-thinking skills. Mastery of foundational math skills is crucial to long-term academic success. Math is a highly regarded content subject area in the educational system and cannot be slighted. In order for a student to have long-term math success, there are basic math fluency skills that need to be learned at a young age. This starts with learning the numbers and counting and advances to more complex math concepts.

Teaching students to become critical thinkers is mandatory for them to be college-, career-, and entrepreneurial ready by the time they graduate from high school. Success in college and the workforce is reliant on this skill and all that it encompasses. Strong reading comprehension, mathematical skills, emotional intelligence, and adaptability make up the premier proficiencies that are needed for student achievement. While they may be more readily associated with academic achievement, these proficiencies also demonstrate social development, which is needed to create vitality in schools.

Student Behavior

Social Behavior

From the time a child is born, behavior is learned, which is why a child's formative years are so crucial to how they will behave when they enter school. The behaviors and skills learned in the home will show up in the school setting, both the good and the challenging. Students who have learned positive social behaviors prior to entering school—such as good listening skills, the ability to follow directions, and good manners—will be more successful in school. Assisting a child or young adult in their social development is just another part of the educational process. Educators pick up from where the parents leave off and hopefully the parents will continue to enhance, monitor, and manage children's positive behaviors. While children are at school, teachers support their social growth and maturation. When a child has not learned basic social and behavioral skills prior to entering school, it slows their development. Educators are then charged with not only the task of teaching those basic behavioral skills, but also correcting the behaviors and habits that impede the learning process, all while teaching academic skills.

Ideally, every child would come to school ready to learn. But that is not always the case. Students come to school with varying issues and behaviors. Positive social behavior is critical to maximizing a student's academic performance. When a child displays what could be perceived as poor or inappropriate social behavior, it is difficult for them to maximize their academic success. A student who has challenging behavior may perform well academically, but they are not fostering their academic growth. The goal is for all students to expand their academic and social potential. Working with parents to address, and hopefully correct, concerns on poor social behavior is going to promote student growth. Supporting the growth and development of all students is key. It requires that educators meet all students where they are, without judgment, and with the intention of helping them grow.

Peer Pressure

All too prevalent in school settings, peer pressure can be negative or positive. Students who do not have the foundation that comes from being part of a strong family are susceptible to succumbing to social pressure. Peers have the ability to alter a student's confidence for better or worse. Creating a classroom environment where students look to positive role models among their peers is one way to improve student learning. Discussing peer pressure with parents and students can help keep students from succumbing to it. Classroom culture is an important part of learning, so educators should encourage student behavior that contributes to a culture of positivity.

Mental Health

The dynamics of education change with every generation. Today, there are social and emotional concerns that must be considered in the process of educating students, which makes mental health an integral part of the educational experience. The mental health of students is as important as their physical health. Mental illness can have an adverse effect on a child's behavior and academic performance. There are many mental health conditions that can impact children; however, anxiety and depression are two of the prevailing disorders we are seeing in our youth. The causes of mental health disorders can be traced to family history, environmental stressors, or psychological trauma, to name a few. Mental illness is a serious issue, and it is particularly difficult for children to manage and articulate what is happening to them. It is up to the adults in a child's life to recognize signs of mental illness and take action to seek professional help.

Other Social-Emotional Considerations

In addition to mental illness, other factors that are of a sensitive nature can surface in the educational setting. Changes in family dynamics can affect a child's mood and behavior—encompassing a wide range of events such as divorce, marriage, the birth of a new sibling, a traumatic experience, homelessness, violence, abuse, neglect, etc. These issues show up in the child's behavior, appearance, health, and conversation, to name a few areas. Being observant and in tune with each child or young adult will increase the chances of detecting a student's need or cry for help.

Home or other environmental factors that have a harmful effect on students could require educators to address the issue with parents or guardians. Parents might be uncomfortable discussing family problems, so it is important to approach these scenarios with extreme caution and sensitivity. Parents might also approach teachers, administrators, or other staff members for support or resources. Schools should partner with outside mental health organizations to provide students and families with referrals when needed.

Mandated Reporter

The safety of students is of utmost importance to schools. Students spend a significant amount of time at school, and educators are responsible for caring for students during school hours. Educators are legally and morally liable for the well-being of the child at home and at school. To ensure the overall safety of students, local and federal laws have appointed educators as mandated reporters.

A mandated reporter is legally required to report any suspicion of child abuse or neglect to the appropriate authorities. Each school has procedures and protocols in place for employees to report cases of potential abuse or neglect. There are various types of abuse: physical, emotional, and educational. These situations can be sensitive and tricky. In many cases, determining if a child is being abused is not black-and-white. There are sometimes gray areas that create uncertainty and doubt for educators, but it is always best to err on the side of caution and make a report if the child could potentially be in mild or severe danger. If it is suspected that any child is a victim of any form of abuse or neglect, it is imperative for educators to report it. It could save a child's life. A child may not communicate that they are being abused or neglected, but there are often other signs that speak for the child. Student safety is always the business of schools and school leaders.

Conclusion

The cycle of life must be factored into our pursuit of social and economic progress, on both a national and international scale. Children are our future and will ultimately inherit our labor and love of life. They will either contribute negatively or positively to the productivity of their generation. Their natural curiosity and innocence predispose them to learn, create, and meet with undefined success. The broader context of their life experiences will either ignite or thwart their creative energy.

Children come into the world as inquisitive intellectuals, natural sponges for learning. They gain knowledge through their inherent curiosity, and learning becomes as natural as breathing. When the minds of children are nourished, they expand. Lack of academic achievement indicates that something is wrong; someone or something is preventing growth. If children are not progressing academically at a steady rate, they struggle to flourish. When students struggle academically and socially, educators and parents must delve deeper to unlock the reasons for any discrepancies in learning and maturation.

Students spend the bulk of their days at school, Monday through Friday. The adults that they interact with most are their teachers and other educational leaders. These individuals serve as guardians of student safety and well-being. Many students need to connect with their teachers or other staff members at school; however, they don't have the maturity level to articulate their wants or needs. At whatever level those connections are established, they are vital to a student's academic success. Teachers are more likely to get students to learn and grow socially if they have built rapport with them.

There are so many factors that affect or influence student achievement, both academically and socially. Student personalities can provide insight into their lives and help educators learn how to support individual needs. Educators can also detect potential mental health or other social-emotional concerns that might impact student learning. Once concerns have been assessed and a plan is made to address them, the goal is to prepare students for college and career upon exiting high school. This demands critical thinking, which relies heavily on the language skills: reading comprehension, writing, listening, and speaking. High emotional intelligence and adaptability further strengthen a student's critical-thinking skills and equip them to be successful in life.

Students are the future. As our world evolves (politically, socially, technologically, etc.), our schools must evolve at the same rate. Students are products of the current world and culture. Educators need to frequently monitor the world's current and changing dynamics to serve children well. Every educational sector (public, public charters, private, parochial, independent, home-school, etc.) needs to consider the impact of social, economic, political, and technological influences on students' academic and social growth and development. All students should be welcomed in any school and seen through loving eyes. Those who were called to the field of education must release any and all prejudices and racist beliefs to have a profound impact on the children and young adults in the educational setting. School is a home away from home where students need to be loved and accepted. Educating all students with *love* is always the right thing.

CHAPTER SUMMARY

- Everything about an educational institution must be designed with the student in mind.

- Student personalities offer insight on performance and motivation, helping educators identify how to address student needs and support learning.

- Helping students develop a positive self-image will assist students to move toward their potential.

- Whatever a student's personality, if they are unmotivated to learn, continually disruptive, or reluctant to engage, educators have an obligation to assess the situation to see if there is a bigger social or emotional issue that needs to be addressed. *All students* have the potential to achieve growth.

- Students with special needs are an essential part of the student classroom population. All students deserve a high-quality education, and this value is reinforced when students with an IEP are included in the least-restrictive environment that will support their academic and social-emotional growth.

- Students who enter the U.S. educational system with a native language other than English make up a significant portion of the U.S. student population.

- Teachers of ELL students should cultivate positive, supporting relationships with students and be culturally responsive.

- Preparing students for the current digital and information age requires critical-thinking skills.

- Metacognition is important for students to become strong readers and critical thinkers.

- Reading is the most crucial component of academic success and the skill that provides a foundation for all learning.

- Individuals with a high emotional intelligence are aware of their emotions and can manage them with maturity.

- The formative years of a child's life are critical to the development of social behavior and determine how well a child will adapt when they enter school.

- The mental health of students is as important as their physical health. Mental illness can have a negative impact on a child's behavior and academic performance. While there are many mental disorders that children deal with, anxiety and depression are the most common.

- Changes in family dynamics can affect a child's mood and behavior, ranging from life events such as divorce, marriage, or the birth of a new sibling, to more traumatic experiences such as homelessness, violence, abuse, neglect, etc.

- To ensure the overall safety of students, local and federal laws have appointed educators as mandated reporters. A mandated reporter is legally required to report any suspicion of child abuse or neglect to the appropriate authorities.

- All children need to feel loved in the educational setting. Only when a child's social-emotional needs have been met can they engage in learning at their highest potential.

CHAPTER 7

Teachers

The Heart of Education

"I think the teaching profession contributes more to the future of our society than any other single profession."
—JOHN WOODEN, *former UCLA basketball coach*

Teachers are the heart of education. They are the breath that keep schools alive. Teachers are society's first line of offense to produce citizens who will have a positive impact on the world. More importantly, teachers are on the front lines of education to secure our country's social and economic growth. The weight that teachers bear is heavy—and often undervalued by the general public. It is the calling on a teacher's life that allows them to withstand the social, emotional, mental, and physical demands of the profession. When they are obedient to their calling and steadfast in their commitment to educate, they can transform the lives of students.

We have to be mindful that schools are facilities for learning, but they also serve as safe havens for students. When students come to school, they need to feel safe physically, mentally, and emotionally for real learning to occur. The classroom is where students seek comfort, acceptance, knowledge, and safety—and teachers set the tone and create the energy that students feel when they come to school. The energy and excitement that a teacher brings into the classroom is critical to student engagement. Students feed off the enthusiasm that teachers bring to their instruction and practice. Teachers have the power to build a student up or tear them down. It is imperative for teachers to be conscious of this and use their power for the greater good of facilitating the success of *all students*.

Teacher Personalities

Every teacher is unique in their personality, and what they offer their students is what makes them special. However, this dynamic can be both a gift and a curse. The approach that teachers bring to their classroom will determine their effectiveness and the impact they have on students and the school culture. As with parents and students, knowing the different personality types for teachers can offer insight into how they can be most effective in creating an environment for students to learn and thrive.

The Alchemist

The Alchemist is a magical teacher with special qualities and skills; they are gifted in a way that can seem uncanny at times. Like an angel sent from heaven, the Alchemist makes use of an elixir that transcends educational theory. Alchemists have all the ingredients of a great teacher. They go above and beyond the call of duty to connect with students, and they possess the magic pixie dust that entices children to learn. Their classroom ecology conveys their passion for educating students, both in organization and execution. Students sense this passion, and it creates a synergy in the classroom. The Alchemist teacher is self-directed and committed to doing a great job. They know that who they are as a teacher will reflect on the school and its administration, and they want to be seen in the best possible light. They don't worry about what others are doing, nor are they associated with drama or negative energy. The Alchemist teacher invests energy into each and every child in a way that conveys their professionalism and humanity. They care about transforming the minds and lives of *all students*. Inspirational and exceptional, these teachers are understandably difficult to find. School administrators need to utilize Alchemist teachers as mentors for new and struggling teachers to replicate the passion and gifts that this kind of teacher brings to the classroom.

The Enthusiast

Enthusiast teachers enter the profession with true enthusiasm for educating students, but they may or may not have the skills to successfully manage the day-to-day responsibilities of being a teacher. They come to work day-after-day with a positive attitude, energetic about the work that they do; however, they are not always effective. Further complicating things, they are usually unaware that they are struggling. In many cases, the Enthusiast has the qualities required and the potential to become a good teacher with guidance. For this to happen, they need to be receptive to constructive criticism and make a concerted effort to develop and grow in their profession. Unfortunately, some Enthusiast teachers are not responsive to coaching and advice. They feel their approach is successful because they are well-liked by students.

While the Enthusiast has great energy and enjoys teaching, their instructional practices do not support student learning—ultimately compromising student achievement. When Enthusiast teachers dedicate themselves to improving their instructional practice, they are worth investing the time and energy to support. However, if they do not show signs of progress over a year's time, they need to be replaced. Close observation of the Enthusiast teacher to assess what is causing them to be ineffective can be used to create a detailed strategy to support ongoing instructional development.

The Minimalist

The Minimalist teacher does just enough to keep their head above water and avoid getting fired. Administrators face a tough decision on whether to keep the Minimalist on staff because while they are not considered good teachers, they are not necessarily bad. They get the job done but not in a way that is impactful to the work of educating students. Administrators struggle with terminating a Minimalist teacher because the shortage of good and great teachers makes letting go of the Minimalist a gamble. They never know if the replacement teacher will be an improvement. The administration should try to develop the Minimalist in hopes that they will take their instructional practice and work ethic to the next level. If that fails to remedy the problem, administrators need to assess the situation thoroughly and release the Minimalist from their employment. Ultimately, if the Minimalist is not committed to growth and excellence, the school will not be able to maximize its impact on students and achieve its mission and vision.

The Run-of-the-Mill

Lackluster teachers are a dime a dozen, ranging from average to below average. They are not "bad" teachers per se, but they don't add value to the school. Run-of-the-Mill teachers are comfortable with being ordinary. In fact, they do not want to take on extra duties or stand out in any way, positive or negative. They just want to exist unbothered. They have mastered the craft of being conventional and rudimentary. These teachers do not like change because it forces them to step out of their comfort zone. As technology advances, these teachers are slow to evolve. Unfortunately, schools are riddled with Run-of-the-Mill teachers, making it difficult to create a great school since they are such a dominant force.

Run-of-the-Mill and Minimalist teachers share similar characteristics in that they are both average in their practice and comfortable with that status. They share a similar lukewarm energy and status quo mindset. The difference between the Minimalist and the Run-of-the-Mill teacher is in their intention, style, and approach to teaching. Run-of-the-Mill teachers are more committed to the profession, as they plan on someday retiring from the classroom. When administrators build positive relationships with these teachers and leverage their commitment, Run-of-the-

Mill teachers can ultimately become good, and sometimes even great, teachers. Minimalist teachers do not put much energy in the profession and are more likely to leave the profession if a perceived better opportunity comes along. There are some Minimalists who are willing to grow, but the difficult conversation needs to happen. When administrators have a positive relationship with teachers, it helps make the conversation less awkward.

The Authoritarian

Often labeled as "strict," Authoritarian teachers are best suited for higher grades. Certain student personalities have a difficult time engaging with strict teachers. When Authoritarian teachers are assigned to work with younger students, their "strict" personality will draw complaints from both students and parents. Oftentimes a strict personality is interpreted as being mean. Teachers who are strict keep a structured, orderly classroom. They need structure, order, and control to function as a teacher. While there are some parents who want their kids to have strict teachers, other parents are uncomfortable with that personality characteristic. Further complicating the matter, some Authoritarian teachers have a hard time connecting with parents. To be successful, Authoritarian teachers need to balance their approach with a soft tone and warm delivery. These teachers can be effectively coached to become "warm demanders."

Warm demanders are teachers who hold students to high standards. They convince students that they have great minds and earn their trust to get them to learn. Close observation of this teacher in action is needed to pinpoint specific characteristics of their style that are particularly difficult. Then a prescription to soften their approach can be offered. The authoritarian approach is not necessarily bad; in fact, it can be quite effective when students know that the teacher genuinely cares about them. For example, if the Authoritarian style consists of a strict daily structure that students are taught to follow, it must also include an ongoing effort to make caring connections with the students. Bringing both a rigid structure and a stern personality to the classroom doesn't work and is not healthy for the social-emotional development of students.

The Hitchhiker

Teaching is a profession that tends to attract individuals who are passing through en route to the profession that they ultimately plan to pursue or to meet the requirements of a loan forgiveness program. The field of education is not their final destination, and they might not even have a destination in mind. Because Hitchhiker teachers are not committed to the profession, their effectiveness is inconsistent. They possess similar qualities as the Minimalist, doing just enough to avoid getting fired. Hitchhikers lack the passion needed to impact students and the ability to contribute to the mission and vision of the school.

The Hitchhiker should be replaced by individuals who are passionate and committed to the educational profession. During the interviewing process, it should be easy to detect a Hitchhiker. The signs should be apparent in their application, résumé, work history, and their responses during the interview. For example, if their work history shows that they have a serious interest in acting, they may be committed to that field and be using the educational profession as a placeholder until they get the right acting gig. If they somehow get hired, they should be replaced.

The Lame Duck

The Lame Duck teacher is an unfortunate case of someone who entered the profession with rose-colored glasses only to find a completely different reality. The Lame Duck has a difficult time managing the dynamics of teaching. While they are well-intentioned, they are in over their heads. They are individuals who enter the field of education with a desire to do good things, but they do not have what it takes to be an effective teacher. It is best to be open with the Lame Duck and release them from their teaching position. Not only does this decision minimize any setbacks to student achievements, but it will also hopefully lead this individual to find their authentic purpose in life.

The Dojo Downer

Teachers who dwell in negativity are Dojo Downers. These teachers are programmed to put a damper on any situation, and they often put others in a sour mood. Left unchecked, they can create a toxic environment. What is worse, they will try to get others to embrace their negative energy. Whether conscious or unconscious, Dojo Downers need the affirmation of other people to survive because only when someone else is unhappy do they feel heard and seen. Dojo Downers often lure unsuspecting colleagues into their clutches under the guise of friendship. They then use the relationships as an alliance for their negative agenda. Positive people are repelled by negative people; however, when negative people join forces, they can coexist and amplify their misery.

Ultimately, it requires a united front to keep a Dojo Downer from spreading toxicity in and around the school environment. Colleagues can subtly diffuse their toxic energy by counteracting their negative comments with positive ones. Dojo Downers will usually get the hint if no one jumps on their bandwagon. Friendly colleagues can encourage the Dojo Downer to be more positive or optimistic. The administrator is obligated to make this teacher aware of their negativity and explain the impact it has on the other staff members and the school culture. When discussing negativity with a teacher, it's fully appropriate for an administrator to make it a lesson in personal growth. Should the teacher be open to it, having a positive attitude will be a life-altering experience, both at work and in their personal life. Be mindful that a Dojo Downer can quickly transform into a malignant teacher, having a lethal effect on the school's program. In these situations, the teacher should be released from their position. Negative people will always derail the school's mission.

The Chicken Little

Chicken Little teachers have similar characteristics to the Dojo Downer; however, this type of teacher is less harmful in terms of their potential to damage the culture of the school. Because Chicken Little believes "the sky is falling," they are fixated on the worst-case scenario and prone to create drama. They feel threatened by changes in procedures or processes. Providing Chicken Little with the facts and breaking down the reality of the situation could lessen the trauma to help this teacher see things a little more clearly. Making Chicken Little aware of their state of mind could create a change and minimize the stress and strife that they experience as they navigate the tides of teaching.

The Diamond in the Rough

New teachers face a huge learning curve. Surviving the "fire" in the first few years of teaching requires tremendous resilience. There are so many moving parts, and new teachers will struggle to manage all that the position entails. It takes a special kind of person to be able to meet all the challenges and demands of being a first-year teacher. When assessing a first-year teacher, there are so many factors to consider: knowledge of subject matter, classroom ecology, organizational skills, communication skills, passion for teaching, and, most importantly, a willingness to learn and improve. The Diamond in the Rough teacher possesses all of these qualities. They are confident and do not require a lot of oversight. They take the reins and move forward, overcoming any challenges that they encounter. To develop this gem, another teacher needs to take them under their wing and mold them into a great teacher. The Diamond in the Rough teacher has the potential to become an Alchemist.

The Toy Soldier

These are substitute teachers who take their place as a warm body in the classroom, either in a short-term or long-term capacity. The Toy Soldier knows that their situation is temporary; they are simply trying to maintain until the end of their assignment, whether it is the end of the day, week, month, or year. This teacher is not necessarily passionate about education. Sometimes they are like Hitchhikers, just teaching until they get to the job they're ultimately seeking. Toy Soldiers are not beneficial to any school. They do not add value. If the Toy Soldier teacher is in one classroom for a long period of time, it can be detrimental and set back students academically. All schools need substitute teachers, but best practice is to hire substitute teachers who are retired teachers or those who are working toward becoming a teacher. Regardless, thought and care should be given to the process of hiring, especially for long-term positions.

Teacher personalities are a key factor in shaping the effectiveness of the classroom experience for students and the undercurrent of school culture. Understanding the different teacher personalities is key to building a dynamic teaching team. Some personalities are open to growing and becoming better, and it's up to the administrative leaders to help them recognize opportunities to get better. Teachers should also be aware of their own teaching personality as a way to self-reflect. Once a teacher identifies his or her teacher personality, it can assist them with their professional and personal growth. It will allow them to determine areas of strength and weakness, contribute to the culture of the school, and impact student learning and mental health.

For better or worse, teachers play a vital role in achieving the school's mission and vision. There are some personalities that will not work if educational leaders are serious about building great schools. Assessing and identifying each teacher's personality at the school site is critical not only to the school's culture, but also to maximizing each teacher's impact on the academic and social development of students. When the attitudes and personalities of teachers and staff align with a passion for education and a desire to help all students achieve, a positive culture of personal and professional development will open new doors. Creating vitality in schools requires a great mix of teachers who add value to the school.

Three Marks of a Great Teacher

What makes a teacher extends beyond personality to include knowledge and formal training, internal motivation, and drive. When an individual decides to go to school to become a teacher, the learning model that colleges and universities subscribe to spans educational theory and practicum. A teacher's internal motivation and drive are revealed in their acquisition and application of knowledge, which is theory and practice. There is another component of a teacher's makeup that is almost equally important—it is what I call *crescendo*. A great teacher will be strong in all three areas: educational theory, practicum, and crescendo.

Educational Theory

Individuals who aspire to teach and work in the field of education are taught educational theory to better understand how people learn. It provides insight on how educators should design, develop, and deliver instruction. The dominant learning theories that are taught and practiced in the education discipline include: behaviorism, cognitivism, constructivism, humanism, and connectivism. Theory can be compared to the skin or outer layer of teaching and the teaching practice. Theory makes up the bulk of the education and training for those who are studying to become a teacher.

Practicum

Most colleges and universities save the practice, or practicum, for the tail end of a teacher's educational experience. It is this part of the teacher preparation where students work in a public-school classroom under the guidance of a credentialled or certificated veteran teacher. This is where student teachers put educational theory into practice. Practicum is a very important part of teacher training because it is hands-on experience in implementing lessons coupled with observation and professional feedback from an experienced educator. If educational theory is the skin of teaching, the practicum phase of teacher development is the bones of teaching.

Crescendo

Aspiring teachers are required to learn educational theory and complete their practicum in order to become certified as a teacher. However, there is another component to teaching practice and teacher embodiment that is rarely discussed. This component cannot be taught at the university or learned while student teaching. It effectively predicts a teacher's innate ability to transition from education theory and practice to the classroom with the knowledge and confidence to be successful—what I call the crescendo.

The crescendo is the instinctive and innate X-factor, transcending knowledge and practice. It is that unexplainable quality that can't be taught in a university course. The crescendo represents the soul of a teacher and how they show up in their educational practice. Educators have a Crescendo Aptitude (CA), on a scale ranging from 0-10. If a teacher has a CA of zero, the likelihood of them becoming a great teacher is slim. An educator with some level of CA can improve with effort on the part of the teacher. In fact, crescendo automatically grows stronger in teachers who possess it. Teachers who enter the profession with a high CA are self-aware; they have a strong feeling of self-efficacy and are self-reflective. They take the initiative to strengthen *both* their weaknesses and strengths. Teachers who enter the profession with a high CA are great teachers in the making. Alchemist teachers have a high level of crescendo. Lame Ducks have zero crescendo. Other teacher personalities can be anywhere on the CA spectrum.

I	I	I
0	5	10
Lame Duck		Alchemist

Regardless of the teacher's personality, education, crescendo, and experience, all teachers need to implement components of effective teaching.

Components of Effective Teaching

Professional Appearance

Professional appearance speaks to the school's brand. If you step into several classrooms across the nation, the teachers' physical appearances will span from extremely casual to casual-professional. It is often argued that teachers should be more casual in their appearance because they have to be on their feet all day, and, in some cases, they are working with small children. What constitutes professional appearance in education is subjective and, without clear or strict guidelines, it is left up to the interpreter. The truth is that the school culture is going to dictate the degree of professionalism required or desired in terms of appearance. As a base level of professionalism, teachers should be clean, and tops should cover the shoulders, midriff, and back area. Bottoms for both men and women should not be shorter than 1-2 inches above the knee. Casual dress shoes are an appropriate professional style. The dress code should be thoughtfully considered, explicitly communicated, and regularly monitored.

Classroom Environment

To have a positive classroom ecology, teachers must be aware of and in tune with everything in the classroom environment. According to Bermudez and Hatkoff, classroom ecology can be defined as all interactions between teachers, students, curriculum, and the classroom environment, which contribute to students' learning experiences. Classroom ecology can be productive or toxic. Teachers can use their presence and classroom culture, climate, physical layout, routines, norms, expectations, language, etc., to cultivate a productive, anti-racist classroom ecology that limits the need for discipline policies.

There are several components that contribute to positive classroom ecology, and they all work together concurrently. Teachers must use their senses in the classroom to coordinate the best classroom experience. The most effective classroom environments include: a clean classroom, organization and structure, clear guidelines, effective instructional practices, student engagement, and, most importantly, safety. Classroom ecology is more about the interaction with the classroom environment. It involves creating a space that supports student learning and student success.

Classroom Cleanliness: The physical appearance of the classroom impacts the mental and emotional state of students, parents, and anyone who enters the room. A classroom environment that is clean and organized creates a space for minds to learn. When the classroom space is pleasing to the eye, it minimizes the distractions and allows for students to focus on learning. A clean classroom speaks to the professionalism of the teacher. It shows that the teacher takes their job seriously and that they want students to feel comfortable and at ease in their learning environment.

Organization and Structure: Creating classroom feng shui involves organization and structure. These are pillars of the classroom environment. In order to maximize effectiveness, teachers must be organized. The systematic arrangement of the classroom reduces the potential for confusion and chaos that can erupt with disorganization. The physical setup and flow of the classroom should support the routines, policies, and procedures of the classroom.

Clear Guidelines: Part of the ecosystem of the classroom are the guidelines and expectations in behavior and classroom etiquette created by students and teacher. Once decided upon, these should be visibly displayed and referred to as needed. The expectations and procedures should be consistently implemented. Clear, consistent guidelines set the standard and tone for the classroom functionality and operation. When students respect rules and procedures, they will contribute to positive classroom etiquette.

Effective Instructional Practices: Instructional practices are another key component to creating the optimal classroom environment. College coursework largely consists of education theory, which teaches future teachers how students learn. Understanding how students learn helps to determine instructional practices. Effective instructional applications engage and motivate students to learn. When teachers use best practices that engage students' senses and emotions, they can maximize student potential.

Student Engagement: Students learn by engaging in their classroom and through a teacher's commitment to instruction. Student engagement can be both active and passive. Active engagement is apparent when students raise their hand, ask questions, respond to questions, participate in class discussions, take notes, etc. Passive engagement shows up in a student's body language, maybe an expression of attentiveness or a light in their eyes. In order for a student to learn, they must be personally invested in the instructional process. Their interest and motivation during instruction and learning is important to their success. Classroom teachers must have an energy about them that draws students into each lesson. Teachers have to be strategic in how they plan and deliver their lessons, channeling an energy that exudes confidence and excitement for the material. The rapport between teacher and student plays a major role in student engagement. When students are drawn to their teacher and there is a positive relationship, a teacher will be more successful in engaging students on a daily basis.

Setting up a positive classroom ecology is quintessential to be effective and maximize instruction and student learning. This is Teaching 101. Poor classroom ecology ultimately impedes the school's progress toward its mission and vision. Administrators and lead teachers must focus on this part of teacher assessments. Good and great teachers innately understand the importance of positive classroom ecology and develop their own style of teaching that incorporates the necessary strategies to successfully administer daily teaching practices that support student engagement. All teachers at each school site must perfect this area of teaching to create the synchronicity necessary for grade-level instruction.

Communication

A major part of classroom ecology is effective communication with both students and parents. The home-school connection is the cornerstone to maximizing student growth both academically and socially. Building positive relationships with parents supports the classroom goals and school vision. When teachers, administrators, and staff connect with parents, it creates a pipeline to student success. Whatever the format (conference, call, letter, or e-mail), communication has to be thoughtful and strategic. Educators must remember, "It's not what you say; it's how you say it."

Language is amazing. It is an art expressed in written form, spoken verbally, and communicated through the physical body. Beauty can be created through language. But language also has an ugly side. It can evoke emotions of anger, sadness, hostility, cruelty, or unpleasantness. Developing the skills and intention to communicate with parents and students in a way that is caring, empathetic, honest, and sensitive to the situation at hand helps to build a connection that is respectful of the other person's feelings.

Communicating with parents about their child's behavior should always start with positive observations about the child before discussing what may be perceived as negative. These comments should be worded in a way that is not harsh or abrasive. When having repeated conversations with a parent about their child's behavior, a special effort should be made to contact the parent when the child has a good day or does something positive. Removing negative words or phrases (no, not, can't, should not, don't, neither, never, no one, nobody, none, nor, nothing, nowhere, etc.) from written and verbal communication can soften the tone of the delivery. There is a skill to constructive communication that takes into account how word choice, sentence structure, and the tone of the written or verbal communication sound to the recipient and what emotions it may evoke. Speaking to students also warrants the same care and intention.

Example 1:
Susie did not attend class today.
vs.
Please be aware that Susie was absent from class today.

Example 2:
Johnny did not get credit for his work because he did not complete his classwork today. He was busy talking to his friend and disturbing the class.
vs.
Please be aware that Johnny received a zero on his classwork today because he was distracted during class and failed to complete and turn in his assignment.

The tone in the examples are different. The messages that include negative language, and that are shorter in length, are more abrupt and come off abrasive. The second sentence in each example requires a little more effort to construct, however they are softer in tone and less hostile. The care that is taken to communicate constructively and to listen well to both students and parents often makes the difference between a positive and negative relationship.

Human Connection

The way that teachers communicate with students and parents will determine the human connection. The teaching profession is a matter of the heart. It does not matter what race, color, or creed—the human connection should trump everything. At the end of the day, students just want to know that their teacher genuinely cares about them. Connecting as humans is built through positive communication and caring interaction. When students feel that their teacher genuinely cares about them, they respond accordingly and are more engaged. When a student speaks highly of their teacher and enjoys going to class and learning, parents typically like the teacher without ever having met him or her. The parent feels a connection with the teacher through their child. That human connection builds trust and brings a mutual respect to all parties involved. The relationship causes parents to respect the work that the teacher is doing and support their efforts throughout the school year.

Annual Phases of the Teaching Cycle

The Annual Phases of the Teaching Cycle

Teaching is a very demanding profession. Supervising and instructing 25-35 students, 5 days a week, sometimes per class, is a huge responsibility. There is variety in each day, week, month, and year. Predicting the unpredictability of student behavior is what creates uncertainty and variation in the daily norm of teaching. The daily challenges and rewards, setbacks and breakthroughs, frustrations and inspirations are all part of the teaching profession. Educators are tasked with serious work—the gravity of being responsible for the daily safety of other humans and contributing to a student's future. All of these teaching duties and responsibilities evoke a range of emotions throughout the school year that can feel like an emotional roller coaster.

The Annual Phases of the Teaching Cycle encompass the emotional, mental, physical, and spiritual feelings throughout the school year. These feelings are driven by anticipation, bliss, climax, fatigue, and renewal. At the inception of the school year, teachers are likely to feel anticipation and at the end of the year, renewal. Teachers experience the phases differently depending on the variables that they are confronted with each year, but the cycle repeats itself year after year.

Anticipation

Preparing for a new school year sparks a feeling of anticipation for what the year will bring, arousing feelings of excitement and/or nervousness. Teachers know that they will have a new class with different students and parents, and all of the unknowns play into that anxiety and excitement. The anticipation phase looks different for teachers, depending on their experiences. Veteran teachers experience the anticipation phase at a different level than a new teacher. A new teacher has a more heightened level of nervousness, excitement, and sometimes fear. The degree of each emotion in this phase depends on the teacher, their experience, and their personality. This phase persists until the bliss phase begins.

Bliss

Two months into the school year, teachers typically find their flow. The teacher knows the students and they have settled into the routine of the classroom structure and style. Teaching and learning are in sync. During this phase, teachers are in a good place. The nervousness and anxiety have subsided, and they are enjoying the teaching process. Students are responding to the classroom ecology, and the rudimentary instruction of procedures are no longer necessary for the most part. The teacher can somewhat relax and coast to the next phase.

Climax

Midway through the school year, teachers hit a climax, or an emotional resolve. By this time, teachers have decided if the year is good, bad, or indifferent. They start to feel the peak of the year and begin to prepare for the end of the school year. The climax of the school year is like inhaling—taking in all that has happened and feeling all that the year has brought to that point. The climax is the high point of the year. During the climax, the emotions from the anticipation and bliss phases are a thing of the past, and there is a vision cast for the remainder of the school year.

Fatigue

The end of the school year brings a new set of challenges for teachers. Students are getting restless and feeling the excitement of summer. It can be a struggle to execute strong instruction in these last two months of school because students are tired and mentally and emotionally preparing for the summer. The calendar is often filled with events, activities, and projects that teachers and students need to address. The mental, emotional, and physical fatigue can take its toll on the teacher. To finish the year strong, teachers must push past the fatigue and focus on the renewal that comes at the end of the year.

Renewal

The renewal phase begins on the last day of school, after the students are dismissed for the summer. This phase of the teaching experience feels like exhaling, a release of all that has occurred during the year. On the last day of school, there is a heightened energy that is released by the students. Teachers feel the students' energy and excitement that occur on the final day of the school year. There is a bittersweet feeling for teachers as students depart for the summer. However, it is a time of renewal. Teachers can step back from teaching to reflect, relax, and renew for the next school year. This is a time for personal growth, which prepares them for professional growth in the next school year. The renewal phase is critical to the teaching cycle because it allows teachers to evolve, and it sets a positive tone for moving into the new school year more confidently, with new and improved strategies and a new level of personal and professional awareness for teaching and learning.

Every year teachers move through these emotional, mental, and physical phases. There is a natural flow to each and a process to be completed each year. When a teacher gets stuck in one phase or the flow of the phases are stifled, it is often a result of challenges experienced on the job. For a new teacher, it could be that they are not growing at a rate that is necessary to keep pace with the job requirements. Getting stuck in a phase could also be due to a difficult student or several difficult students. Sometimes the flow of the teaching phases can be impeded by a teacher's personal life. If there is something that is challenging a teacher in other areas of their life and they cannot separate their professional life from their personal life, it could be an inhibitor. Teachers should take note of these phases and how they move from one phase to the next. If they are not moving, they should investigate why and resolve the problem in an effort to get to the next phase and complete the cycle.

Administrators and parents should be cognizant of these phases and support teachers throughout the year. Creating vitality depends on keeping the energy alive, and teachers can more readily do this when they know that they are valued. Schools that are focused on vitality need to put customs and traditions in place to celebrate teachers and show them that they are loved throughout the year. A small token of appreciation goes a long way. As a standard and norm, teachers should be acknowledged on birthdays, around the holidays, and during teacher appreciation week. In addition, the Parent Teacher Association (PTA) can take the lead in affirming teachers with monthly teacher appreciation motivations to acknowledge teachers more regularly for their work and dedication to the profession. These rituals and celebrations support teacher rejuvenation throughout the year.

Self-Care

Teaching is a very rewarding job, but there are challenges and stress that come with the profession. There are so many hats that a teacher must wear that it is easy to become mentally, emotionally, and physically drained. As the school year progresses, the risk of burnout increases, ultimately threatening teacher performance. It is important to put strategies in place to minimize the stressors teachers face.

Teachers can take their mental health into their own hands by being well-organized and prepared daily and by maintaining positive classroom ecology. Creating routines, policies, and procedures for students and parents to follow will minimize the uncertainty of each day. It is up to the school administration to create a culture of positivity so that teachers feel good about coming to work each day. Over time, this reduces stress and supports a more joyful environment for everyone.

Teachers need to establish a positive and encouraging support system with their colleagues. Teachers who band together to complain and spread negativity are toxic for each other and the school. Teachers should shy away from any negative colleagues; they are wolves in sheep's clothing. Complaining and negativity undermine the work environment and have the potential to make life and work a living hell. It will not only affect one's professional life; it can also impact one's personal life. It is crucial that teachers are surrounded with positive people who have their best interests at heart and support their efforts to be better in all areas of their life. Banding with positive colleagues is critical to self-care. Everyone creates their own experience, but a group determines the work environment. Each teacher has a choice and should accept personal responsibility in protecting the mental and emotional space of the work environment.

Beyond the work environment, teachers need to find ways to decompress outside of the school site. Regular physical activity such as fitness classes, cycling, yoga, and hiking are known to support both mental and physical health. Self-care requires that educators maintain the balance that sustains mental health.

Conclusion

At the end of the day, teachers make the magic happen. They are with students for the bulk of the day, and they have a tremendous impact on a child's academic, social, and emotional development. As a child moves from one grade to the next, one school to another, each teacher steps in to be a lifeline for that student, facilitating their development. The hearts of teachers are connected to the students they meet. When teachers interact with students, they must see the students' potential and prepare them for who they can be, not for who they are at the time of introduction.

Administrators need to be in tune with the influence teachers have on students at every school site. They are special beings, and their work is meaningful. We cannot discount teachers and the impact they have on students and, ultimately, society. Creating vitality in schools can only happen with a team of people who are willing to evolve and grow to support student needs. Like students, adults are works in progress. Teachers who are willing to grow and be better every year are worth the investment.

Teaching is a matter of the heart. It is not relevant what color, race, or creed the teacher brings to the classroom—their passion, dedication, and love transcends all else. Students have an opportunity to experience humanity at its best through the love of their teachers. A teacher's impact extends far into the student's future, however positive or negative it may be, which is why selecting the right teachers is so important. Understanding the different personalities found in schools will help to create vitality of the classroom environment. Teachers must be willing to grow as educators. They must also reflect on how their classroom practices and personality traits contribute to the educational climate and efforts to work toward access and equality for all. As we begin the healing process, teachers have the ability to take the lead and be pioneers for change.

A Teacher's Morning Affirmation

*Today I will make a difference in the lives of **ALL** of my students. I will encourage and motivate them to be the best that they can be!*

*Teaching is my calling and my purpose in life. I will be obedient to the calling. I will serve in a way that elevates **ALL** of my students and colleagues. I will serve as a light of love and humanity.*

CHAPTER SUMMARY

- As the heart of education, teachers keep schools alive.
- When students come to school, they need to feel safe physically, mentally, and emotionally for learning to occur.
- The impact of a teacher, good or bad, extends well into a student's future, which is why selecting the right teachers is so important.
- Teacher personalities impact their effectiveness and how successful they will be in developing their students.
- The components of effective teaching include the classroom environment; professional appearance; cleanliness, organization, and structure; clear guidelines; and student engagement.
- Teachers move through the phases of anticipation, bliss, climax, fatigue, and renewal throughout the school year. To best evolve in their profession, they need to complete this cycle.
- A positive work environment and culture helps to reduce stress and support teachers so they can feel more joy in coming to work each day.
- Being organized and prepared every day and maintaining a good classroom ecology will support a teacher's mental health. A teacher's passion, dedication, and love for students transcends all other things, including color, race, or creed.

PART 3
EDUCATION

A Better Future for All

CHAPTER 8

Closing the Achievement Gap

Leveling the Playing Field

"The world as we have created it is a process of our thinking. It cannot be changed without changing our thinking."

—ALBERT EINSTEIN, *German physicist*

The *achievement gap* has been a problem in the United States educational system for decades, and there has yet to be a solution to effectively address and correct the issue. The achievement gap can be defined as the disparity in academic achievement between African American, Hispanic, and Native American students and their Asian and white counterparts. When students are not performing at or above grade level at an alarming rate, we cannot ignore it. The gravity of the problem warrants attention and a concerted effort to correct this disparity. There are several key issues that need to be addressed in order to move the needle and close the achievement gap.

When there is a disproportion in the educational achievement of student racial/ethnic subgroups, it demands the attention of educational leaders, politicians, parents, and society at-large. The nature of the achievement gap classifies it as a social injustice. Education is a legal right for all citizens and residents in America. When black, brown, and indigenous children and young adults are not excelling at the same rate as their white and Asian counterparts, we must recognize that the educational system is perpetuating racial inequality. Rethinking the approach to alleviating the racial inequality that shows up in the achievement gap shows good faith that America is moving in a direction toward social justice and breaking down the structural barriers that have prevented African Americans, Hispanics, and Native American people from attaining a life that is freely available to other Americans as a right and a privilege.

Closing the Achievement Gap

For years, educational leaders have focused on closing the achievement gap, but there has been little to no progress to show for it. There has been so much concentration on and energy directed toward the problem—the name itself is centered on the problem, the gap, as opposed to the desired results, the academic achievement of students of color. It is time for educators to divert their attention and energy toward the desired results. Moving forward, emphasis and strength should be given to Equitable Educational Success, the ultimate goal. Shifting the focus from the problem to its solution transfers energy toward the desired result.

Equitable Educational Success is the process by which parents, students, educators, politicians, and society at-large work collectively toward the academic success of African American, Hispanic, and Native American students, thus closing the achievement gap. There is a universal understanding that what you focus on is what you get. If there is a continued focus on the gap, it will persist. Past leaders who have had the biggest impact on the world through social justice movements put their emphasis on what they wanted to achieve instead of focusing on what they did not want. Take Dr. Martin Luther King, Jr., for example. He fought against hate, violence, segregation, and inequity using strategies that were innately opposite of those he fought against. He fought violence through non-violence; he fought hate with love. Dr. Martin Luther King, Jr. made a lot of monumental changes during the Civil Rights Movement because of his strategy and approach to justice for people of color and humanity. The achievement gap speaks to stagnation, and Equitable Educational Success speaks to progress. There must be a strategic plan to have a positive impact on education for all children. The educational movement that we are experiencing will ultimately become a socioeconomic movement. Both will start with the push for Equitable Educational Success.

Equitable Educational Success

We are all in this together. Education is a pillar of progressiveness in society and for humanity. As such, there must be a cooperative effort to ensure that *all* students, including children of color, are afforded a quality education that allows them to compete both nationally and globally as adults. Educational leaders have a professional responsibility to support the goals of Equitable Educational Success. There is a social responsibility that politicians, community leaders, organizations, businesses, and society must own in leveling the playing field for students of color through education. Last but not least, there is a personal responsibility that parents and students must take in order to become a part of the solution. Equitable Educational Success is a collective effort, and all parties must engage in order to achieve the desired results.

Professional Responsibility

Education is a calling. It is a profession of passion and service, one that is committed to the responsibility of providing *all students* with a quality education. It is a unique career that holds the future of individuals, ethnic and cultural groups, and the world in its hands. There is power and responsibility involved in being an educator. Educators have a moral and ethical duty to maintain high standards for themselves and their students. They must be passionate, purposeful, thoughtful, and intentional in the work that they do. Their work must be guided by a vision of the desired success of their schools and students.

All students have to be a priority. Disparities in academic achievement among racial subgroups have to be addressed to create balance and to level the playing field for the future of *all* students. From there, educators are responsible for ensuring that inherent racial biases do not lower the standards and expectations for students of color and the quality of education that they receive. All educators, including administrators, counselors, the dean of students, support staff, district officials, and governing board members, need to shift their thinking and response to students of color to affirm equity, access, and fair treatment in every decision. This requires that educators acknowledge and understand the issues and concerns that contribute to the achievement gap.

An educator's job is no longer just about academic development; it is about developing the whole child. A child's development includes nurturing and understanding all areas of concern, including social and emotional issues that impede learning. The whole child has needs beyond academics, which must be addressed. School and education are such a huge part of a child's life, it is not uncommon for families to seek support and resources from the school. When family matters hinder the child's social, emotional, and academic growth, the instructional work of educators often takes a back seat. To address mental health issues and social-emotional challenges effectively, it is essential for parents to work in partnership with the school to attend to a child's needs.

Considering and understanding the historical journey of students of color in the American educational system is another key to reversing the damage that has been done and to changing the trajectory of these students. By looking at the past, educators will uncover the inherent racial biases that have shaped their thinking and influenced how they engage students. Educators must commit to rethinking and reimagining their approach in providing a quality education for all students. For example, who can take honors, AP, and advanced math classes? Which students get access to the best teachers? How are students suspended based on their infractions? Can students get access to information in the language that is used to communicate with them at home? Educators must let students know that they are intelligent and valuable and make them aware of resources that will benefit them both in the present and in the long-term. Regardless of the challenges students of color might face, there needs to be a continual push for early literacy and a commitment to putting students on the path toward college.

Due to the long, dark history of racism in America, a norm has been created surrounding racial biases and the treatment, expectations, and social position of people of color. There has been an ingrained and subconscious perception of their fate. Professional responsibility requires a conscious effort to reverse what has become systemic in the American educational system: ill treatment of groups of people who have been forced into a place of disparagement. The history of education in America tells a painful story of the fractured relationship that people of color have had with educational institutions and the generational trauma that has been perpetuated as a result.

Racism and Education in America

African Americans have suffered a long history of being enslaved, both physically and mentally, in America. As slaves, it was against the law for Black people to learn to read and get an education. As the country made efforts to evolve economically, it became divided on how best to use slaves (Black people) for labor. The government eventually decided to free slaves, at least on paper, to advance the industrial movement. Following the Emancipation Proclamation, anti-literacy laws for Blacks remained in place both in the Northern and Southern states. Jim Crow laws were created to enforce racial segregation in the south and to prohibit African Americans from having full access to their rights as citizens of America. The battle for African Americans to exercise their rights as outlined in the 14th Amendment spanned several decades, from Plessy vs.

Ferguson in 1896 to Brown vs. Board of Education in 1954. But it did not stop there—the long history of keeping African Americans mentally enslaved through anti-literacy tactics continues today. African Americans continue to fight the good fight to exercise their rights as outlined in the U.S. Constitution.

Native Americans experienced a different journey than Black people that resulted in the same fate. British colonizers used education to assimilate Native Americans into European culture. The government removed indigenous youth from their homes and placed them in boarding schools. The Native American boarding schools, or Indian Residential Schools, stripped Native Americans of their culture. They were forbidden to speak their native language or use their native name, and they were forced to cut their hair. Laws were created to enforce the government's plan to assimilate and denigrate the indigenous people. The government used religious organizations that employed unethical and degrading methods in the guise of providing a basic education to children. The last boarding school of this kind was closed in the 1970s. Native Americans had to fight to take back their mental and physical freedom from the government.

Mexican Americans became the subjects of European colonizers during the Mexican-American War, which ended with the signing of the Treaty of Guadalupe Hidalgo in 1848. The treaty awarded the colonizers possession of a large part of Mexico. The treaty allowed those living in the acquired land, both Mexicans and native people, rights as citizens. The treaty stipulated that Mexicans could continue to speak in their native language, Spanish. However, later laws were enacted to prevent students from being taught in their native language. In 1946, the court case Mendez vs. Westminster ended school segregation in California. This case was a stepping-stone for the decision in the landmark Supreme Court case Brown vs. Board in 1954, which declared that separate public schools for Black and white students was unconstitutional, overturning the Plessy vs. Ferguson decision in

1896, which declared segregation constitutional if schools were "separate but equal."

The fight for equity and equality in education continues to this day. The current state of education carries undertones of this dark history and reflects the modern-day version of anti-literacy laws to ensure that people of color do not have the ability to progress and achieve the American Dream. Educators changing how they think and act on issues of race in education is an individual effort on behalf of the group. Every educator must address their own conscious and unconscious racial biases and correct how they see, support, and educate students of color. This requires that they show empathy and make sure that actions and decisions are not to the detriment of students of color, while at the same time considering the mental and emotional trauma that continues to affect these students and their families today. It's the professional responsibility of educators to provide these students with a quality education, correcting the trauma that has been inflicted on their ancestors, which parents have passed down to their children, making their educational experience a generational curse.

The Collective Effort to Reverse Racism

People of color remain marginalized through education—or a lack thereof—by design. Education has been used as a tool to suppress African Americans, Hispanics, and Native Americans, from exercising their legal rights to their full potential. Anti-literacy laws and segregated schools have prevented people of color from having equal access to a quality education. More importantly, it has mentally conditioned people of color to view education and their relationship with educational institutions negatively. Educators whose classrooms include African Americans, Hispanics, and Native Americans have an obligation to correct the past and make room for the advancement of people of color through educational reform. In order for the educational system to be redefined in America, it is going to take more than the work of educational professionals. The long history of systemic racism is a huge undertaking; however, the process must begin to affect change. Reversing the effects of racism demands a collective effort.

Social Responsibility

Even today, educational institutions continue to perpetuate systemic racism. Schools have minimized and marginalized the advancement of people of color, both inadvertently and overtly, and the achievement gap proves this reality. Today, the appearance of education is misleading. There are shallow conversations and false attempts to support students of color through ineffective programs. Education is a fundamental right for all who reside in the United States. A change in the foundation of education would play a major role in initiating social equality for *all students*. Society needs to accept responsibility to ensure Equitable Educational Success for children of color.

In addition to this being a social responsibility, there is an ethical and moral obligation for individuals, politicians, nonprofit organizations, corporations, and community leaders to work toward eradicating the educational injustices of inequality and social biases directed at students of color. This social responsibility needs to include discussions, efforts to advocate for equity, and actions taken to achieve social justice for students of color. These actions can come in a variety of forms like volunteering, charitable giving, educational policies, partnerships, funding, etc. Laws that promote and enforce social justice in education will have a huge impact on Equitable Educational Success and will initiate a movement that will change the current educational paradigm. This shift will have a profound impact on both students of color and our country as a whole.

Personal Responsibility

Equitable Educational Success cannot overlook the personal responsibility of parental involvement and student engagement. Parents have a personal responsibility to make education a priority in the home and to engage in their child's education. Working in conjunction with schools and teachers is critical to attaining Equitable Educational Success. This starts with early literacy, the foundation to the development of strong reading skills. Before a child enters school, parents have a duty to provide their children with primary literacy skills. Once the child enters school, parents need to work collaboratively with the teacher to further develop the student's reading skills and ensure that they are reading at grade level or higher. There are myriad resources that parents can access to support their child's early literacy skills.

Furthermore, parents have an obligation to seek support when needed. Regardless of the family dynamic or situation, parents must push past difficulties and rise to the educational challenge to position their child for long-term success. Parents cannot allow circumstances to prevent them from prioritizing education. Parental involvement is key to Equitable Educational Success. Establishing an expectation for a minimum level of parent involvement is the first step. The next step is for schools to create ways for parents to take action and engage with their child's education. The culture of the school will dictate the best approach for parent engagement in support of the school's efforts to achieve Equitable Educational Success.

While parents are the driving force for a child's academic success, students also have a personal responsibility to exert a maximum effort toward their academic growth. Personal engagement and effort put forth toward academic progress and development assists students in their long-term success. Prioritizing education, reading, and learning will ensure that they have the skills they need to excel in all academic subjects. Making education a priority is a simple practice that can be achieved by reorganizing how time is spent each day. Reading should be a daily practice in an effort to foster a love of reading and build strong reading comprehension skills. Ignorance imprisons the mind while knowledge is liberating. Personal responsibility translates into personal power.

To create great schools that are focused on vitality, there has to be a plan for building Equitable Educational Success. African American, Hispanic, and Native American students are groups that are negatively affected by the achievement gap, and they represent a significant number of students who are reliant on the public education system. A quality education applies to *all students*. Any plan toward Equitable Educational Success for students of color will undoubtedly benefit all children and society-at-large.

Conclusion

To the naked eye, the current American educational system appears to have evolved from its past. The truth is that it is definitely different but still offers students of color more of the same. The achievement gap is the result of the systemic racism still prevalent in education in America. Breaking down the racial infrastructure is the only way to build an education system that reflects Equitable Educational Success for students of color. Educators must understand that unavoidable life challenges are compounded for African American, Hispanic, and Native American students. There is an added stress that comes with being a person of color in America. There must be a consideration for the extra burdens placed on individuals of color. Having empathy and consideration for the weight that these students carry helps to lighten the load. Moving toward a more humanistic society requires empathy. Education is an ideal place to begin the healing process and start reversing the damage. Through education, we can ultimately help remove the added stress felt by students of color and support Equitable Educational Success for all students.

The achievement gap describes a problem that has persisted for decades. Equitable Educational Success describes the solution to correct the gap. Educators, politicians, parents, and students need to change how they think about the achievement gap. The focus and energy of the efforts to close the gap must concentrate on the goal and not the problem. By continuing to focus on the achievement gap, we are going to get more of the gap instead of its closure. Moving forward, if everyone takes collective responsibility for establishing Equitable Educational Success, our efforts will speak to and put energy toward improving the academic success of African American, Hispanic, and Native American students. Embracing a new mindset will give educators, parents, and students an opportunity to envision the possibilities of a brighter, more equitable future.

CHAPTER SUMMARY

- The achievement gap has been a prevailing problem in the U.S. educational system for decades, and we have yet to find a way to effectively address the problem.

- Disparity in the educational achievement of student racial subgroups should command the attention of educational leaders, politicians, parents, and society at-large.

- Education is a legal right for all citizens in America and when black, brown, and indigenous children and young adults are not excelling at the same rate as their white and Asian counterparts, we have to recognize that there is an element in the educational system that speaks to racial inequality.

- To change the focus of efforts to empower students of color, it's important to work towards the goal of Equitable Educational Success rather than closing the achievement gap.

- Education is a pillar in a progressive society. As such, there must be a cooperative endeavor to ensure that *all students*, including children of color, are afforded a quality education that allows them to compete globally as adults.

- Understanding and considering the historical journey of students of color in the American educational system will enable the work that must be done to reverse the damage and change the trajectory of their future.

- There is a social responsibility that politicians, community leaders, organizations, businesses, and society must own in leveling the playing field for students through education. Educational leaders have a professional responsibility to support the goals of Equitable Educational Success. Finally, there is a personal responsibility that parents and students must take in order to become a part of the solution.

CHAPTER 9

The Pandemic and Education

Change Is on the Horizon

"All great changes are preceded by chaos."

–JOHN MAXWELL, *American author*

I n March 2020, the COVID-19 pandemic took education by storm. When it was deemed a global health crisis, the United States went on lockdown with little warning. Residents became subject to an unprecedented nationwide quarantine. Education was shook. All of a sudden, schools were compelled to shift from physical classroom instruction to distance learning. Around the country, school-aged children were forced into a virtual learning environment that relied heavily on parental support and guidance to be meaningful for students. The pandemic thrust parents onto the front line of their children's education.

The abrupt change in the learning environment from school to homeschool was different from school to school and home to home. It required a physical, mental, and emotional adjustment for teachers, parents, and students—and it affected everyone differently. Some people were able to get on board with relative ease, while others struggled. Initially, it was believed that students would return to school within three weeks, but three weeks came and went. The pandemic took a turn for the worst. The number of people who were testing positive and dying from the virus increased. Schools were mandated to remain closed until there was a marked decline in the number of people testing positive for the virus. Most of the country was on lockdown due to state-imposed stay-at-home orders, and the uncertainty of schools reopening became a controversial subject for politicians, parents, students, educators, and the public at-large. School closures continued through the end of the 2019-2020 school year. Proms and graduation festivities were canceled, and students struggled to accept the fate of their social and educational milestones. The crisis continued into the summer and the uncertainty of the reopening of schools in the fall created angst and fear for parents, students, and educators. Education was in limbo. The political leaders of each state were compelled to make decisions based on the guidance of the Centers for Disease Control and Prevention (CDC). As a result of the uncertainty and health risk, school closures persisted into the 2020-2021 school year. Distance learning continued, and there were grave concerns about the student learning loss and the health and safety of the public moving forward.

Despite the craziness of an unprecedented pandemic, there were clear takeaways for education. Moving forward, education has to consider and address the impact of the pandemic and school closures on education and students. There are advantages and disadvantages resulting from the pandemic and the implementation of distance learning. Some have already played out, and others are either less obvious or remain to be seen.

Distance Learning

Many people believe that the COVID-19 pandemic created an educational crisis. Still, others believe that it was a turning point, a defining moment that revolutionized the way teachers teach, students learn, the role technology plays as an instructional and learning tool, the way parents engage in their children's education, and the value placed on teachers.

The pandemic challenged and changed education in a variety of ways. Prior to this global event, home-school and online classes were a choice for a select few. When the novel coronavirus hit, remote learning became mandatory for every student from kindergarten to college. Everyone was compelled to acclimate to this new educational format on short notice. By and large, the majority of people were able to adapt to the circumstances. To some extent, it showed teachers, parents, and students that they were capable of rising to the challenge. It also showed that the collective efforts of teachers, students, parents, and the community are pivotal to the success of schools and student achievement. It solidified the idea that we can all be better if we work together.

When school closures were mandated, the educational platforms that were used to deliver instruction virtually were implemented at varying levels, depending on the schools' level of adaptability and resources available to launch the curriculum virtually. The closures caught schools off guard and, as a result, distance learning was a model that most educators, students, and parents had to figure out in real time. Initially, it proved to be a minimally effective undertaking for most schools. However, by the fall of 2021, the learning curve to understand and work with the virtual platforms flattened, and most schools were better prepared to take on the task of teaching students virtually. There was a lot of information gathered from the initial experience with distance learning, and educators had time to wrap their heads around the dos and don'ts of remote learning and how to move forward better and more effectively. Remote learning is still relatively a new concept, so educators, students, and parents are continuing to learn what it means for students now—and what it will mean in the future. As the country cautiously moves back to in-person instruction, distance learning could become obsolete. Fortunately, significant improvements in technology over just a few months have also made a difference. Technology was already important to education, but in the pandemic, it became an essential tool for teaching and learning. Everyone involved in the educational process was required to keep pace with the ever-changing technological improvements.

155

Distance learning did present some challenges for parents and students. Some parents had a difficult time supporting their child's education at home without becoming their child in the learning process. In some cases, it became easier for parents of younger children to feed their child answers to class activities, assignments, and tests. However well-intentioned this was on the part of parents, it was to the detriment of the child's learning and progress. Other parents did not have the capacity to support their children at all. There were a number of students who disengaged from the educational process completely during distance learning. On the return to in-person instruction, the damage caused by distance learning began to be revealed. The fallout has yet to be fully realized, but there is an undeniable increase in the number of students who are behind academically—and those who were already behind are likely to regress even further.

Student and Parent Engagement

A huge drawback to remote learning is the inevitability of learning loss. Many students were lost during distance learning—an inescapable horror due to the lack of engagement, devices, and connectivity. Educators were required to address the issue of accountability and student engagement, which, in turn, shifted the nature of classroom structure and management. The new learning environment presented educators with so many variables that were outside of their control and previously not a factor in in-class instruction and learning.

African Americans, Hispanics, Native Americans, and students from low-income households were cornered by the pandemic. COVID-19 not only attacked these populations physically, it also negatively impacted learning for students in these groups. Traditionally performing behind the curve academically, students of color were further impacted by the global health crisis. In the battle to close the achievement gap, there was no room for the pandemic pause that ensued—resulting in the interruption of progressing reading and math skills during the quarantine and distance learning. A staggering number of Black, Hispanic, and Native American students disengaged from education during this time. It is a reality that comes to the detriment of both these students and public education as a whole. While technology could do little to help these populations, it proved to be education's saving grace in the pandemic.

Technology

Technology is a beast that has taken over our personal, professional, and social lives. It dominates every industry and controls how we do business. Technology dictates the status of our economy, global development, and progress as a society. It is advancing exponentially faster than any other molecular component or creation. Technology continues to adapt and reach new levels of capacity at an unstoppable rate. Education, like every other industry, has been deeply affected by this technological typhoon. Over the years, public education has been slow to fully embrace and implement new technology due to a variety of reasons, not the least of which is funding. Other educational sectors have embraced technology more readily and advanced accordingly since they are more closely aligned with available technology.

The health crisis propelled teachers, students, and parents into full-on adoption of educational technology. When it came to remote learning, adaption was the name of the game. The pandemic offered no other alternative. It was sink or swim, succumb or succeed. Educators, students, and parents had to decide to what extent they were going to participate in distance learning. Depending on their unique teacher personalities and technological competency, educators engaged with distance learning at varying levels. Alchemist teachers were quick to get on board and transition to distance learning and work toward its full potential. Other teachers resisted by either retiring or leaving the profession. Many teachers became Minimalists, learning just enough to keep their jobs and keep up with daily instruction. In the wake of the pandemic, technology created both utopian and dystopian realities in the field of education.

Technology Utopia

The surge in educational technology in response to the pandemic has empowered educators to create a paradigm shift in their traditional mindset of teaching and learning. Teachers were forced to set aside antiquated thinking and experience the power of technology in education. In the digital age, the benefits of educational technology are undeniable. It improves and enhances a student's critical thinking and prepares them for college and career. Online assignment submission and real-time visibility of graded assignments and assessments also come with advantages. For one, online assignment submission reduces the use of paper and time spent copying. The enhanced accessibility of shared teacher resources improves instructional practices across the nation and globally. Teacher innovation and creativity is also sparked by technological advancements, and the list goes on. Broader implementation of technology in education provides many benefits that far outweigh the pitfalls or shortcomings.

Technology Dystopia

Distance learning was both a gift and a curse. Although distance learning allowed schools to continue educating students virtually, there was also a digital divide that prevented some students from accessing the curriculum. There were students who lacked the connectivity required to engage in distance learning. There were parents who did not have the mental and emotional capacity to support their children with distance learning. These families were engaged minimally or not at all. Teachers, students, and parents who were intimidated by technology struggled to fully participate. Teachers who had a difficult time adapting to the technology that was required for teaching and learning during quarantine were not able to maximize their instructional practices and, as a result, students could not maximize their learning. Remote learning required all parties involved (teachers, parents, and students) to become proficient with a new educational platform.

In general, the reliance on technology has reduced human connection, creating isolation. Social media and gaming had already been contributing to isolation among youth; educational learning via technology has added more to that already pervasive problem.

Human Connection

In education, people are our greatest and most precious resource. Regardless of how advanced technology becomes, human connection will always be of value and will be a necessity. Online and virtual learning allowed education to continue, but the human connection was threatened, and that proved to be a huge concern for everyone. The social and professional disconnection was initially a challenge when the school closures started, but as it continued into the next school year, the human connection between teachers and students evolved into a different, meaningful form for many.

The Alchemist and Diamond in the Rough teachers—teachers with a high level of crescendo—were able to create and maintain connections with students virtually. Their energy, effort, and passion for teaching translated. There is a clear understanding among educators that in-person class for most students is the optimal learning environment; however, we know now that any future pandemics or crisis that requires school closures will highlight that educators who are meaningfully engaged and passionate about the work they do will masterfully engage and connect with students as effectively online as they do in person.

As schools transition back to in-person classrooms, many students will need some time to feel at home at school. Connecting with teachers and peers will take a little more time and effort than it did pre-pandemic because students are relearning how to interact with people. There will be a new appreciation for in-person instruction and the human connection because of the value it adds to the lives of students. Likewise, teachers who are passionate about their job and who were affected by not having an opportunity to interact with the students in person will appreciate connecting in person again.

The human connection of teachers in the classroom is invaluable. Schools are a safe haven for many students. There are so many variables in the home that have negative and positive impacts on students. School offers students some separation from home life, which can be important regardless of the circumstances at home. Schools are an integral part of children's lives, as are teachers and other educational leaders at school sites. They serve as an added layer of protection and comfort for students that cannot be replaced by technology or any other mechanism or device. It is important for society as a whole to focus on preserving human connections as we progress into the digital age and rebound from the pandemic. It is vital to protecting and strengthening humanity.

Pandemic Predicaments

The pandemic exposed the character of every individual, their work ethic, and who they are at their core. Some people saw an opportunity to grow and become better, to progress, while others took it as an opportunity to cut corners and do as little as possible, regressing. The field of education experienced a similar divide in the attitude and work ethic of employees thrust into a digital environment. When education transitioned to distance learning, there were teachers who maximized teaching and learning. They worked overtime and challenged themselves to provide high-quality instruction to engage student learning, while others compromised on quality, engaging less with students and working less. This same phenomenon applied to staff members and parents. School closures and remote learning led these individuals, Distance Learning Drones, to relinquish their moral responsibility to educate students to the best of their ability. Similar to a Toy Soldier, they adopted a poor work ethic that was detrimental to student achievement.

It was disheartening to see the number of drones that emerged during this time. Nevertheless, the pandemic forced parents and teachers to work together for the greater good of the students. Many schools saw the partnership between home and school strengthened during the mandatory quarantine. This is momentum that can be used to improve schools. The impact of the COVID-19 pandemic on education presents a unique opportunity, a catalyst for much-needed change.

Education has a lot to consider as it moves beyond the pandemic. The post-pandemic phase presents more uncertainty, uncharted waters that will impact students both negatively and positively. The vitality of schools will fall to school leadership, the decisions that are made, and the implementation of practices and policies.

The pandemic has changed the way industries do business, and education is no exception. Technology has revolutionized how we do education both now and in the future. So, what does education look like past the COVID-19 pandemic? The transformation of education is underway, and a new direction is in sight.

Future Educational Models

Distance/Remote Learning: Distance learning has been a part of education for some time in the form of online courses, homeschooling, etc., but the pandemic officially introduced it to households across America when students could only attend school virtually. Through distance learning, students receive instruction from their teacher remotely via an electronic educational platform, either at home or some other location away from the classroom setting. Up until the pandemic, students and parents were given an option to either pursue in-person education or homeschooling. In March of 2020, distance learning became the only option for students in grades K-12 in most, if not all, states. Beyond the pandemic, public schools could give students an option to attend school either in person or virtually. This will give students who prefer the homeschool model an opportunity to participate in the social components of traditional school (i.e., sports, clubs, etc.). This idea remains to be seen. However, if nothing else, remote learning will be a viable option and solution to any future crisis or pandemic.

Hybrid Educational Model: The hybrid educational model reflects a combination of remote and in-person classroom instruction and learning. Students attend school in-person 50 percent of the time and distance learning 50 percent of the time. Students attend class in-person on select days of the week and attend class remotely on the other days. The hybrid educational model will be a viable form of education as the country fully recover from the health crisis. This educational model has afforded schools a way to navigate learning in a crisis.

In-Person Educational Model: Conventional education has relied on the in-person educational model, in which students participate in instruction and learning by attending class. In the traditional educational model schools are facilities for instruction and learning, teachers are the primary instructional facilitators, and parents offer additional support for teaching and learning. This model has long been the most desirable form of education until the pandemic required distance learning. There are still many parents who prefer an in-person education model that allows their children to be at school all day, 5 days a week. Parents who desire in-person learning over the other educational models also maintain that schools contribute to their child's academic and social development in a valuable way that other models can't replicate.

The pandemic presented what seemed to be an impossible challenge to traditional, in-person education. Educators, students, and parents were introduced to a new way of education and gained a new perspective on how students can learn in a non-traditional educational model. Educational models were not the only areas of society affected during the quarantine. Social and political unrest erupted, compelling educators to address racism, race, equity, and access in schools and the classroom.

Racism, Race, Equity, and Access

Racism is a virus that continues to plague our country. The onset of the COVID-19 pandemic was compounded by the murder of George Floyd at the hands of Minneapolis police officers. The event reminded Americans of the hate, ugliness, and inhumanity that racism breeds. In 2020, a montage of phone video footage showed unapologetic white privilege culminating in a modern-day public lynching. It was racial discrimination at its worst. George Floyd's murder and the events that followed sparked protest and demonstrations around the world. All races and genders united in a call for change, a world where people are united by their shared humanity. For that to happen, everything needs to be laid out on the table—racism, race, equity, and access—to make a plan to eradicate racism and to put that plan into action. Education will play a huge role in contributing to the larger objective by tearing down the walls of systematic racism in schools. There needs to be a radical change in how human development is approached for racism to be destroyed. In the school setting, this must start with leadership.

Leadership

School closures altered the dynamics, roles, and responsibilities of educational leaders. The confines of leadership were immediately expanded beyond the school gates and into the homes of students, teachers, and staff. Going forward, leaders will need to understand the new role they will need to play as they lead outside the boundaries of the school site.

Post-pandemic, educational leaders will need to be courageous and willing to break the mold of tradition. Current leaders need to embrace this paradigm shift and begin thinking about how to address racism, race, equity, and access. They will have to get comfortable with being uncomfortable in conversations about race and racism. There must be an intentional effort and ongoing conversation to address how race and racism relate to classroom and instructional practices. More importantly, dismantling racism is going to take the work of educational leaders from all educational sectors (public, private, parochial, and higher education). All educators have to be a part of the conversation and solution. Traditionally, only economically advantaged students were privileged to attend private and parochial schools, but these invisible barriers to access must be challenged in order to ensure that diversity and inclusion reflects all educational sectors. When students of color are pushed out of the private school option, it decreases the opportunity for diversity and racial understanding in these schools. Efforts around equity and access should not be restricted to public schools. These ideals must be applicable to all students regardless of race, color, creed, or economic status. Students of all races must be privy to the dialogue about race and racism in all school settings. Educational leaders will have to prioritize equity and access in their policies, procedures, and school decisions. Leadership will take on a new meaning for educators to implement real change.

Educational leaders will have to spearhead the efforts and changes that take place as we move toward dismantling racism and fostering a society that is united through humanitarian beliefs and actions. Eradicating systemic racism in schools will take intention and tenacity. Confronting the topic of race and racism will be an ethical and moral responsibility not only in conversation, but in practice.

Teacher Training

Deconstructing racism in education is going to require college and university teacher training programs to ramp up and improve their efforts. Through discussion and instruction, educator hopefuls need to be equipped to address equity, access, race, racism, and restorative justice. Developing new teachers in these areas prior to entering the classroom will transform education and traditional practices that perpetuate racism and racial biases. For real change to take place, professional development will have to take on a new focus and format.

Personal Development

Going forward, professional development will have to focus on human or personal development. Dismantling racism starts with the individual's mindset. The common goal of uniting as one race, the human race, begins with individual work to assess personal racial biases—understanding that how you treat someone is not about who *they* are but about who *you* are. In order to treat someone or a group of people better, each individual must reflect on who they are, how they think, and how they interact with people of color. In their work with students, educators need to foster the same personal development. The more one understands themself, the better they can understand others. Newcomers to education can be better equipped if colleges and universities incorporate equity, access, and race into theory and practicum. For both new and veteran teachers, teacher training will need to emphasize self-reflection and self-evaluation. Teacher training as it relates to race, racism, equity, access, and restorative justice will need to be ongoing. The work that needs to be done will require tremendous effort and intention on the part of educators.

Educator Health and Wellness

The COVID-19 outbreak and all of the subsequent social and political distress that occurred during 2020 took a toll on so many people. The field of education was hit hard by the quarantine and distance learning. Teachers were identified as essential workers and were asked to be mentally, emotionally, and physically strong as they supported students and families and the disruption in their own personal lives. Even in the face of fear, stress, and pressure to perform, educators were compelled to push through anxiety, depression, and any other emotions. Mental health will be a significant part of education health and wellness as educators stand on the front lines of dismantling racism. They will need appropriate support to stay strong on their course and quest to educate students and break free from hundreds of years of divisive thinking that has plagued our country and the world.

Education Around Social-Emotional Best Practices

Children and young adults are exposed to so many negative influences. They cannot escape the ascendancy of violence, sex, and social ills. These are highlighted on television, in cartoons, and in all of the places that used to be safe havens from destructive influences that once preserved childhood innocence and encouraged moral and ethical behaviors. Technology and social media have taken on a life of their own, impacting youth in unprecedented ways. The internet allows students to access any information and videos, positive or negative. Social media is inundated with more information and videos while tracking its user's preferences, tastes, and interests to keep them constantly engaged. Social media has become a socially acceptable drug. The users of this deceptive drug are susceptible to mental, psychological, and emotional damage or trauma. This comes on top of any emotional, physical, or mental abuse or neglect that could be occurring in the home. Real life for youth can pose challenges for students as well, particularly for students of color. Racism puts an additional distress or disturbance on their plate.

All of these factors must be taken into consideration as we develop the whole child and support their social-emotional growth, development, and healing. Education will need to consider several factors and implement practices that will address student social-emotional trauma. The practices will need to include supporting the social and emotional health of students in the classroom, on the playground, and in the home. Partnerships with community organizations that specialize in mental health will be extremely important. Being able to successfully connect families with these organizations will build a community of support for mental health and social-emotional support.

Conclusion

To date, the effects of the COVID-19 pandemic on education have yet to be revealed. It will take some time past the pandemic to fully grasp the impact that it has had on students. The pandemic challenged the way teachers teach and students learn. It challenged the way educators think and how they show up in the classroom for students. During the nationwide quarantine, technology saved education from collapsing. Technology was able to create a bridge between the home and school, delivering instruction virtually. Educators, parents, students, and schools were able to unite, shift gears, and transition to distance learning in order to preserve the continuity in instruction and learning. The pandemic revealed that the certainty of educational practices are uncertain.

A culture of vitality is needed now more than ever to account for both the certitude and improbability of education. Vitality will influence the *long-term strategic planning* that provides a blueprint of the road that educational leaders must travel toward achieving the school's vision. Every school's strategic planning should include keeping pace with *advanced technology* as it relates to all aspects of the business, especially with teaching and learning. The perpetual evolution of technology is a major cause for educators and schools to ensure that *adaptability* is a main element in the school's overall practices, among other things. The unpredictability of the direction of our country's social democracy and education's direct connection to *political policies* forces leaders to maintain a pulse on the political climate. The *quality* of schools is contingent upon their level of flexibility and ability to adjust and evolve with the times and in emergency situations that arise with little to no notice.

Educators are now charged with addressing another virus in schools—racism. Ensuring that there is equity and access must be a goal for all educators. It will be through personal development that educators will find the courage to engage in the practice of self-awareness in order to address personal biases, prejudices, and classroom practices that contribute to racism in schools. In the coming years, we will either see educators work to administer a vaccination to eradicate racism or continue to deal with the ongoing crisis of each new variant or strain of our fractured humanity.

CHAPTER SUMMARY

- The 2020 pandemic thrust parents to the front line of their children's education as the learning environment moved from school to home.

- There was a physical, mental, and emotional adjustment required of teachers, parents, and students in the adoption of distance learning, affecting everyone differently.

- Concerns about student learning loss were heightened when school closures persisted into the 2020-2021 school year.

- The pandemic created an educational crisis, a defining moment that revolutionized the way teachers teach, students learn, and the way parents engage in their children's education. Consequently, the perceived value of teachers and the role of technology in instruction and learning skyrocketed.

- Technology became a tool of necessity to teaching and learning. Distance learning technology improved drastically in a matter of a few months.

- The health crisis forced all schools to rely on technology to quickly scale remote learning capacity. Teachers, students, and parents were propelled into educational technology.

- A school's level of adaptability and access to resources and technology educational platforms affected the implementation of remote learning curriculum.

- The Alchemist teachers were quick to get on board and transition to distance learning and explore its full potential. Other teachers resisted the technology, with some choosing to retire or leave the profession altogether.

- A huge drawback to remote learning has been the inevitability of learning loss.

- African Americans, Hispanics, Native Americans, and students from low-income households were hard hit by the pandemic.

- The number of students who disengaged with education during the quarantine and distance learning is staggering, to the detriment of these students and the growth of public education.

- People are the most valuable resource in education. Regardless of how technology advances, the human connection will always be a necessity.

- Teachers who bring energy, effort, and passion to their work (a high level of crescendo) are able to create and maintain human connections with students virtually. The pandemic exposed the character and work ethic of every individual. For many people, it was an opportunity to grow and become better.

- Beyond the pandemic, the vitality of schools will depend on bold leadership, decision-making, and the implementation of practices and policies.

- Dismantling racism requires educational leaders in all sectors (public, private, and parochial) to work together for the solution.

- College and university teacher training programs need to expand their efforts to equip future educators on the topics of equity, access, race, racism, and restorative justice.

- Educational leaders must prioritize equity and access in the policies and procedures of school decisions and directly address the topics of race and racism.

- Education will play a huge role in tearing down the walls of systematic racism. Having important conversations about racism, race, equity, and access—and putting a plan into action—will move the world closer to humanitarianism, the ultimate goal.

- Professional development should be focused on human or personal development because dismantling racism starts with the individual mindset.

- As educators stand on the front lines of dismantling racism in education and the world, there will be a need for increased attentiveness to mental health and wellness.

Summary of Impact

The profession of education is a calling. Those who enter the field of education are drawn to it because they are obedient to their calling and purpose-driven in their work. The nature of the work puts educators in a category all their own, and they are hailed as living angels by many. Being an educational leader is not about power; it is about purpose and influence. The influence of educators has a tremendous impact on the lives of their students and, collectively, it shapes the future of society and the world. Given the seriousness of the role that educators play in society, there is a sense of urgency placed on schools to get it right. So many schools across America are flatlining. There is a pressing need to resuscitate these schools so that they may not just survive, but thrive. Educators need to be equipped with the fundamental skills to build vitality and maximize academic success in our schools. This book has outlined the ingredients and recipe for school vitality. Schools are meant to thrive, and anything short of that is a disservice to children and society. Vitality can only occur when there is purpose and intention in the pursuit of goals that will fulfill the school's vision.

A clear vision is the starting point for creating a great school. Every school must be deliberate in drafting, designing, and implementing steps toward its vision. The vision has to be communicated, supported, and believed by all stakeholders. The stakeholders include administrators, teachers, staff, parents, students, and community partners. Vision is so critical because it provides a blueprint for educational leaders to set goals that are in alignment with the ultimate objective. From there, the right people must be assembled to make the vision a reality.

A major component to the development of vitality in schools is hiring an excellent staff, a Dream Team, that is emotionally connected to the school's vision. It is vital for administrators to be intentional and give extra effort and care to the hiring process. The members of the Dream Team have to be true professionals and possess characteristics that set them apart from the average educator. Leadership needs to seek out qualified applicants and use every part of the interview process to gain information about the candidates. During the interview, the interviewer must rely on the information ascertained from the application, résumé, and letters of recommendation to create a profile of the applicant. Ultimately, it will be the energetic human connection, or lack thereof, that will determine if the candidate is perfect for the position or not. Finding the best person for the Dream Team is going to also require selling the school to the potential employee because strong candidates will have several options. Hiring staff worthy of being on the Dream Team will ultimately make the educational leadership team stronger and will contribute to the culture and the success of the school. Creating the right chemistry among the staff will bring a rhythm to the daily operation. The rhythm will direct the daily flow of staff's coordinated efforts toward the school's vision, as orchestrated by the administrative leader. The leadership will determine the effectiveness of the function and flow of the overall team performance.

Leadership builds capacity and allows employees to take ownership of the role that they play in contributing to the mission and vision of the school. All employees serve as educational leaders at each school site. The Leadership Congruency Postulate explains how every educational leader, regardless of their position, serves as the highest-ranking leader at a given time. Every educational leader must take ownership of their position and show up as an important part of the larger team. Leadership positions are not to be taken lightly. There is a responsibility that should be valued and held in high esteem. Leadership is largely responsible for establishing a standard of professionalism and ensuring that the school functions as a business.

The business of schools is to provide an educational service to students and its stakeholders. Oftentimes in public education, a business environment is overlooked because the service provided is free. The standard and expectation of free service is devalued. In order to elevate the schools' program and work toward the vision, the business model must be to provide excellent customer service. All areas of the daily operation of schools need to play an integral part of achieving the school's goals. To ensure that the service being rendered is exceptional, all parts of the school operation must be held to a high standard. The other components of the school operations include finances, human resources, the governing board, facilities, etc. It is important to know that the principal clients of a school are students and parents. Teachers provide direct customer service to students and parents on a day-to-day basis.

Students are the primary reason why schools operate; however, with the students come the parents and teachers. In the educational system all three of these groups need to work together for the greater good of student growth and academic achievement. All parties share an equal responsibility in the success of the child. If one or more of these parties falls short in their obligation and contribution to the process, the child suffers. Students, parents, and teachers all come to the educational arena with different personalities that define how they approach school and interact with one another. Recognizing the range of student personalities helps teachers and parents work together to support student needs. Identifying parent personalities will help educators communicate better with them and build positive relationships to maximize the desired results. Teacher self-reflection and awareness of their own proclivities facilitates personal and professional growth. As teachers grow personally and professionally, they will be better equipped to support all students and all types of learners. A teacher's impact on students will be determined by their level of commitment to student learning and professional responsibility. Teacher personalities help to define the strength and quality of every teacher. Alchemist teachers produce the best results. Schools should endeavor to ensure that the majority of the teachers at each site are Alchemist teachers.

It is essential that the academic success of *all students* be a priority when creating vitality in schools. Unfortunately, the educational system in America continues to fail students of color. There is a huge achievement gap that continues to put African Americans, Hispanics, and Native Americans at a disadvantage socially and economically. The country's history has placed a dark cloud over the educational structure, and even today schools are consciously and unconsciously perpetuating the hate and fear that our country was founded on hundreds of years ago.

The achievement gap is the direct result of racism, discrimination, and anti-literacy laws placed on students of color. Changing how we view and label the achievement gap is going to drastically change the efforts to close it. It is important to change the focus of education to the desired result versus the existing problem. In moving forward, shifting the focus from the achievement gap problem to the solution, *Equitable Educational Success,* will create hope and progress toward the possibilities of a more equitable educational system. Thinking differently about the problem and focusing more on the solution moves the educational system in a positive direction. Another factor important to the academic success of people of color include the need for educators to understand how the long, dark history of education in America has contributed to the low performance of three groups of students. Empathy and understanding of the implicit biases that have hindered the academic development of students is imperative to reverse the damage that has been done. Achieving Equitable Educational Success will take the work and responsibility of educational professionals, politicians, students, and parents. When a large group of students are not experiencing academic success, they face an even bigger disadvantage when a crisis (such as a pandemic) hits, disrupting services with school closures or distance learning.

The pandemic transformed education. Teaching and learning took on new meaning and form. Parents were compelled to be more hands on with their children's education. Teachers had to learn a new way to deliver instruction and engage students in a virtual classroom. The pandemic presented many challenges for educators, parents, and students. However, there were opportunities and advantages that resulted from the crisis as well. Technology, for instance, was taken to another level. Education had to adapt and evolve to meet the needs of the remote-learning platform. Educators enhanced their technology competence to maximize instruction and learning. Moving forward, educational technology, teaching, and learning will look different as a result of the pandemic. The health crisis proved that educators need to continually engage as a student of their profession, regardless of how they choose to advance in their career.

Educators are facilitators of human psychological, social, emotional, and academic development. As students move through the educational process in their compulsory education in grades K-12, they are at the mercy of educational leaders. Educational leaders are charged with the task and responsibility of producing critical thinkers and leaders who will carry the torch of professional and social advancement, humanity, and love into the future. They play a major role in the progressiveness of our world's social and economic evolution. In order to have a lasting impact on the world, schools must have a model, framework, and philosophy that transcends time and circumstances to create vitality. More importantly, through proper education, educators have the ability to improve humanity around the world.

Vitality is important to the evolution of education because the future of education is uncertain and ever-changing. Regardless of what direction it takes, education will continue to exist because it is part of the fabric of our country and the world. Education provides the training for all other professions, such as doctors and health care professionals, which confirms the fact that educators are essential workers. While the educational movement will undoubtedly change, the principles to creating great schools are foundational and timeless, and they stem from creating and maintaining vitality. There is room for schools to change and progress and remain relevant. Every aspect of the educational process and function contributes to the vitality of schools. There must be an intention to function and operate at a high level and to provide excellent service in the quest to achieve the school's vision.

Education will be an essential part of our world's existence in some shape, form, or fashion for a very long time, and we need to ensure that the progress and evolution of schools keep pace with the ever-changing economic and social movement. The vitality of schools will ultimately be reflected in the economic, social, and humanitarian progress of our society and the world.

"The cave you fear to enter holds the treasure you seek."

—JOSEPH CAMPBELL, *American university professor*

Education in History: Dismantling Racism in Education

"Change will not come if we wait for some other person, or if we wait for some other time. We are the ones we've been waiting for. We are the change that we seek."

—BARACK OBAMA, *44th U.S. president*

American history has shaped the foundation and tone of public education in this country. Like the country's history, education in America is a story of hate, fear, prejudice, and racial divide. History books whisper an account of slavery, boarding schools, anti-literacy laws, discrimination, and segregation. African Americans, Mexican Americans, Native Americans, and other Hispanics have been victims of a social injustice that created a long history of generational trauma. Centuries of mental damage to people of color have been catastrophic. The constitutional rights of these ethnic groups excluded "life, liberty, and the pursuit of happiness." These "unalienable rights" were stripped from people of color as a result of laws and mental conditioning that prevented all but a fortunate few from achieving the American Dream.

The story began hundreds of years ago when Europeans invaded African villages and through violence, abuse, and intimidation enslaved the African people. Almost simultaneously, European settlers landed in what is now called America and colonized Native Indian territory. Two groups of people, two worlds apart, enduring a similar experience. As European settlers expanded their quest for land in America, Mexicans also became subject to their ruthless antics. Once Africans were brought to America against their will as slaves and indentured servants, the experience of all three groups was woven into America's story. The physical abuse was horrendous and inhumane at best, but it was the mental abuse that long outlived the abolition of slavery and segregation. Laws did not impede the goals of the white majority to maintain a superior position in the world. The racial degradation, inhumane treatment, and mental torture was perpetuated through education. The American educational system was an incubator for racism. Educational institutions pushed the government's agenda to support the toxic mental conditioning of African Americans, Hispanics and Native Americans.

European settlers understood the mechanics of the mind centuries ago. They were aware that an attack on the mind would keep the intended groups of people in a subservient position in society. Keeping the mind enslaved would entitle them to a position of supremacy into the future beyond the confines of shackles and blatant racism. Historical accounts lead us to believe that the government's attack on African Americans, Hispanics, and Native Americans was intended to strip them of their humanity. Ultimately, they not only wanted to dispossess people of color of their carnal being, they also wanted to dispossess them of their divine being, the infinite wisdom and spiritual power that lies within *all people*. They used knowledge of the mechanics of the mind to erase the divine identity from people of color through physical, mental, and emotional torture. Depriving them of their human experience and knowledge of their inner divinity, early American colonizers kept people of color in a mental prison long past the abolition of slavery, government-run boarding schools, and segregation. The historical trauma has evolved into a generational curse that has been nearly impossible to overcome, especially in light of how our society continues to be divided. Our failure to see past differences like race have prevented us from understanding that we are all alike in every other way.

As a result, hundreds of years after the abolition of slavery, decades after the Mendez vs. Westminster and Brown vs. Board of Education decisions, education continues to be a conduit to implement oppressive tactics that are designed to prevent the progress of people of color. People of color continue to be mentally incarcerated by way of their ignorance, their lack of knowledge. The fetters have been removed, but the appearance of racial biases have been masked and the mental enslavement persists. So much emphasis has been placed on resources as they relate to equity and access, while neglecting the mental damage that is preventing students of color from accessing a quality education. Great wisdom has proved that a prisoner cannot be released unless they know they are imprisoned. It's time to reverse the generational damage that has resulted from the oppression of people of color. There can be no ceiling on the heights one can climb socially and economically whether in education or any other sector of society—this is the change that desperately needs to take place.

Education Today

When the 2019-2020 school year started, it was business as usual. Students participated with in-class instruction, and traditional education as defined by the turn of the century was in full swing. About seven months into the school year a health crisis struck not only the country, but the world. As students across the country transitioned to distance learning as a result of the COVID-19 pandemic, 2020 marked a pivotal time in history. So much transpired and lives were altered in unimaginable ways. More importantly, the blurred lines of racial inequality in America became starkly black and white. The murder of George Floyd, a Black man, at the hands of a white police officer, exposed the systemic racism that has made up the fabric of American history.

Black people continue to be the recipients of blatant racial injustices and inequality in a country that they helped to build. Our country has arrived at a crossroads in our history where we must decide if we are going to change the narrative of the Black and Brown experience in America or continue to turn a blind eye to racism. Education is critical to implementing the changes that need to occur to advance the Black Lives Matter movement, which promises to have a positive impact on humanity—all people.

Black Lives Matter is not a statement against the lives of others— it is merely a plea for a group of people to become humanized in a country where they have always been "otherized." The movement was initiated on behalf of African American people who were hardest hit, even killed, by structural racism. Black people have taken the brunt of racial and social injustices in America and around the world. (That is not to minimize other groups who have also been marginalized.) The controversy surrounding the statement, "Black Lives Matter," has ignited a chain of rebuttals: "all lives matter," "blue lives matter," etc. These counter statements have sidelined a desperate and sincere attempt to humanize a group of people with a tit-for-tat, painful sarcasm. The irony is that the statement Black Lives Matter would not be necessary if, in fact, "all lives mattered." The Black Lives Matter movement will level the playing field and support the humanity of *all people*. When all people are viewed and treated as equals, we will see humanity at its best. No one is free unless everyone is free.

Schools continue to contribute to structural racism. Structural racism in America uses education to perpetuate the mental and economic genocide that has long been a reality for people of color. For real change to occur, education needs a systematic overhaul. What has been happening for centuries must be addressed in the educational system in order to see real impact in the country at large. There will have to be a seismic shift in higher educational training and personal development to eradicate racial barriers and biases in the field of education. There has been a dehumanizing of Black lives and other people of color that is manifested in the quality of education that they receive. This shows up in the standards that they are held to, the resources that are distributed to their neighborhood schools, and the programs that are created to ensure their demise, like pipeline to prison. The current structures of education have to be dismantled, breaking down racial barriers and biases.

Since its inception, the United States has offered two different educations—one for white children and one for children of color. These two systems deliver very different experiences, an experience of privilege for whites and disenfranchisement for students of color. A bandage has been placed on the deep wounds of racism and inequality. For real healing to occur, our country must take a serious look at the practices used in schools to affect change.

Children of color are vulnerable in the educational system. It is going to take a change in mindset for the educational community—including politicians, administrators, teachers, and staff—to bring about educational reform. Educators have to determine how their own identity (all those things that make up who they are, in all complexity) plays a role in how they show up in the classroom and dictates their perceptions of students. It is a process of self-reflection, self-evaluation, and a conscious effort to eradicate racism from all educational systems. Educators have to see themselves in their students and empathize with children of color who have been marred by racial ills that inhibit their social and economic advancement in the country in which they live. When someone has the ability to see another as they see themselves, shared humanity is the result. An oppressor has the ability to heal their heart and free themselves from the unconscious hatred and fear that penetrates the soul. The liberation of the afflicted automatically emancipates the oppressor from their shackles, and allows them to experience personal growth and expansive love that provides a spiritual freedom that will penetrate every area of their life. Expansive love can only be experienced through humanitarianism. The oppressor has to be willing to walk away from the tradition of racism to be a light for themselves, others, and the world.

A New History for Education

Education continues to create its history. There is a vision and spirit for change. The current state of education is no longer relevant nor acceptable for the educational and economic movement that is on the rise. The world is traveling toward an all-encompassing humanitarianism. It is time to turn the page on racism, prejudices, and division. Our narrative has to be driven by the intention of creating positive change. Breaking down the walls of racism in schools is key to dismantling racism everywhere. Racism is steeped in our culture and tradition, but education is a universal experience. Given a change in the mindset of educators, education has the power to dispel the cultural traditions of racism. Educators at-large have to be willing to be pioneers for the next level of life. An acknowledgment of the educational history of America and how it denied people of color the equal and fair access to a quality education and life is the first step toward healing, recovering, and changing the trajectory of American education for students of color and establishing an educational system that values humanity. Systemic racial inequality can be changed with an intentional effort on the part of those who consciously or unconsciously contribute to its continued existence.

In education, *the greatest impact and contribution we can make toward mankind is love.* Love is rooted in humanity—not just love of some but love of all. Humanity is hindered by racism. By design, racism is hatred, and it results in a social and economic divide. We cannot unite as a human race with hatred and division at the core of our global existence.

Education in America has a long history of laws that prevented groups of people from being educated. Laws and unwritten practices, such as segregation, racial discrimination, and inequity of resources in schools have stifled the educational growth for all children over the years. We are still in the process of repairing the damage of centuries of a broken system that devalued the education of *all children.* Politically, our country has been slow to make the necessary changes to strengthen an educational system that continues to fail hundreds of thousands of children, generation after generation. Educational leaders today are charged with the task of building quality schools.

Education: The Next Chapter

We are at a pivotal moment in history, politically, socially, technologically, and economically. At this critical time, changing the course of education is imperative. If we are going to move in a positive direction as a country, education and humanitarianism have to be at the forefront of the movement. Humanitarianism can only take place in a world without racism and sexism. In order to rid racism from our society we have to take the risk to get to know one another.

Moving forward, education will look different in structure, style, and implementation. Schools will offer more options than before as to how students can participate in their academic and extracurricular programs. The traditional model of in-person class will resume; however, students who excelled during distance learning may want to continue to participate with the distance learning educational model. Parents may also want their children to participate in a hybrid model of education, where they attend school in person part-time and distance learn part-time. For schools to remain relevant and to service the current needs of students, they will need to be flexible in their approach to delivering instruction. The in-person educational model, hybrid model, and distance learning model are all viable options that schools will need to consider to best facilitate the needs of all students.

Educational leadership will need an overhaul. Every level of leadership at districts and schools will need to consist of individuals who are progressive thinkers, consummate professionals, and courageous pioneers. Leadership must confront and address the topics of racism, race, equity, access, and restorative justice and, in turn, dictate how schools and education will evolve and build vitality. Hiring practices must be intentional. A call for strong, quality administrative leaders will be the impetus for the next chapter of education. Leadership must ensure that Alchemist teachers have a dominant presence at each school site, and support staff need to play a major role on the leadership team. Support staff will need to be utilized more effectively and strategically to achieve the mission and vision of the school. Leadership will ultimately be the driving force of change. They will need to bring well-honed leadership skills, a new mindset, and an ongoing commitment to personal development.

Personal Development

To evolve and ensure Equitable Educational Success, schools need to implement a new focus on professional development. College and university training for teachers and administrators must be compelled to design their educator preparation courses to reflect the current educational movement. This will improve the preparedness of individuals who graduate from these respective institutions for the work to be done. District and school site personal development and training should be intentional and ongoing, reflecting the needs of the educational movement. Social-emotional education will be pivotal in addressing the generational trauma created by racism and the current mental health issues that are prevalent among student groups.

Social-Emotional Education of Students

A surge in mental health issues among students, young and old, is a concern for school leaders. Student mental health can improve or hinder the academic and social development for a child or young adult. To develop the whole child, there must be room for mental health support. Having the ability to identify potential mental health needs and connect students and families with the appropriate clinic or resources is imperative. Staff will need to be equipped with the tools to work with students on mental health issues and cope with difficult situations. This weight that educators are asked to carry can be challenging. It is important that their well-being is monitored and considered throughout each school year.

Mental Well-being of Educators

Teaching the future generation of the human race is the highest level of responsibility that one can take on. Educators are essential workers, occupying the trenches to make the world a better place. It's a huge responsibility that involves bearing the weight of others and reversing harm. The gravity of this leadership position tends to place so much focus on the service being provided that those in the position tend to put themselves on the back burner, which can be unhealthy. Providing educational leaders with the knowledge and strategies they need to take to create a mental and emotional balance in their personal and professional lives is vital to the educational movement.

This Is America: A New History is Being Written in Education

Education stands at a crossroads. The ideas, customs, and traditions that have long been the framework of the educational system are being challenged, and there is a desperate call for change. At long last, our society is confronting and questioning the dominant infrastructure of white, male supremacy. America is a multi-cultural and multi-gender society. Its leadership, ideas, and customs must begin to reflect its people. Our nation has an opportunity to lead the way toward global humanity. Change is on the horizon. The world is on the brink of a massive shift. Education can help initiate that shift. Through education the world can evolve in a way that transcends antiquated traditions and unchallenged belief systems.

Educators must lead the charge to dismantle racism and be a catalyst in the movement toward humanitarianism. Almost every person experiences the impact of an educator at some point in their life. Educators affect so many individuals and the ripple effect continues with each student. Educators transform the minds and lives of students through the work that they do, as they are charged with the task to produce critical thinkers and leaders who will carry the torch of humanity into the future. The goal must be to educate all students, including students of color, with love, compassion, and empathy. Equitable Educational Success benefits everyone. Most importantly, it has a profound impact on the movement toward humanity.

A Vision of a Better World

We are connected by our shared humanity. We are one big family. Educators have to be able to see themselves in their students, see their children in their students, and see themselves in parents to achieve the fullest extent of the changes that are needed to modify the trajectory of America's educational history. We are one, and until we see ourselves as one in education, the past patterns and misconduct of racial biases and inequality will persist. If we are in pursuit of becoming greater, we must completely understand that racism is wrong and, for as long as we live in a society dominated by white, male supremacy, we can never be better. It will take a concerted effort by everyone to remove those thoughts, ideas, principles, and practices that hold us back from experiencing our full potential. Understanding that change begins with self-awareness, educators can do the work individually and as a group to deliver results.

Our modus operandi is strictly based on what we have been taught—customs, traditions, and habits. The world benefits from a more open-minded view of humanity. There is so much talent in all of us. When we don't allow others to realize their potential, we run the risk of losing out on great discoveries like inspirational music that could help individuals through tough times; medical research and revelations that could save lives and inventions that could have a profound impact on world progress. Giving every individual an opportunity to create and serve humanity through their gifts and talents is in the best interest of everyone. The possibilities of who we can become as a nation and as a global ally are endless if everyone can free themselves of racial biases and barriers. We can create what our minds envision. Global peace, harmony, and humanitarianism are possible. Living in a world where race, color, gender, and creed don't matter is possible if we believe and do the work necessary to realize that vision. We have to fight the good fight, not just for students of color, but for the sake of humanity. Educators are called to leave the world better than we found it. They must be a light for *all children.*

Appendix A

A Purpose-Driven School: Pasadena Rosebud Academy

"Do not despise these small beginnings."
—ZECHARIAH 4:10, *KJV*

Pasadena Rosebud Academy Charter School was born from a vision, a passion, and a purpose. It was conceived from a strong desire to provide students with the foundational skills that they need to be successful in high school and beyond. The vision was centered around the core principles of critical thinking, financial literacy, travel, global awareness, and service. However simple and sincere this vision was, the road to opening Pasadena Rosebud Academy Charter School was an uphill battle. The journey consisted of roadblocks, setbacks, detours, doubt, and naysayers—and faith and miracles, too.

As the visionary behind Pasadena Rosebud Academy Charter School, I was fortunate to have a small group of supporters who believed in my vision from the start. I was also certain that a higher power was the driving force behind my vision, passion, and determination. Both then and now, God remains at the helm of the Rosebud journey. Along the way I was conscious of His presence and knew that if I did what I could, He would do what I could not. Despite the obstacles, roadblocks, and detours, I had unwavering faith that things would work out, and I used each negative experience as motivation, instruction, and guidance to help me navigate the journey. My faith became as Hebrews 11:1 states, "the substance of things hoped for, the evidence of things not seen." Faith allowed me to persevere through the obstacles and setbacks. Surviving the naysayers and defeating the Goliaths, my faith allowed me and those who were in the trenches with me to understand that opening the doors of Pasadena Rosebud Academy was His plan.

Pasadena Rosebud Academy Charter School is a divine creation. Everything that has transpired prior to its inception to the present day has been in alignment with divine order. In 2005, when I expressed an interest in starting a school, there was a small group of individuals who were committed to my vision, even if it was just to see what would happen. It was an idea that did not really make sense at the time and there was no roadmap to seeing our vision come to life. So, I know that these individuals were in my life as part of God's master plan. During the school planning phase, the goal was to open in September 2007. A year into the developmental stages, we had not been approved to operate, we did not have a location, and we did not have teachers, students, or operating funds. Despite these dire circumstances, we had a burning desire to bring the vision to fruition and open the academy. We continued to pursue what we set out to do without hesitation or discouragement, working through the barriers that confronted us. Fourteen years later, as I reflect on this time in my life, I can see the tremendous courage it took to pursue this vision. As Winston Churchill said, *"courage is going from failure to failure without losing enthusiasm."* We never lost enthusiasm, and we never thought about quitting.

A Guardian Angel

The initial challenge that we faced was getting our charter approved by the Pasadena Unified School District (PUSD), the local school district in which we wanted to operate. In 2006, the year we submitted our petition to operate within the district boundaries, there were two other charter schools petitioning to open as well. Charters were new and perceived as a threat to existing, traditional schools in the district. The district's strategy was to approve two charters and deny one. One school was the favorite and a guaranteed approval. The other school said all of the right things and appealed to the district's political interests. We were the underdogs. We were designated as the school to deny. The other two schools were approved without hesitation. The administrator overseeing the charter petitions, at that time, was determined to block our school from opening. When it was time to submit our petition to the PUSD Governing Board the designated district staff made a recommendation to deny our request.

There was a lot of dialogue and challenging situations that we encountered. In the end, we were fortunate that there was a board member who felt strongly about approving our charter petition and fought tooth-and-nail to ultimately gain the support of three other board members, making four total, just enough votes to approve our charter. He was our guardian angel. Even after this approval, the attempts to undermine the work that we were doing persisted. There was one battle after another and without the passion and determination planted in our hearts, I'm not sure that we could have endured all of the opposition we experienced. Fortunately, we were and continue to be purpose-driven. Although the challenges were difficult, they never deterred us. Once we were approved, the real work began.

Walking by Faith

Throughout the journey, we walked by faith and not by sight. Purpose-driven by a higher power, we were never discouraged and never wanted to quit, even when times were challenging and things looked dire. There was a driving force that was beyond our control. We could not turn back even if we wanted to. Every aspect of the journey was carefully and divinely orchestrated.

The first teacher I hired was Teresa, a former student of mine. Two years prior to the opening of the school, I happened to run into her in the community, and she mentioned that she was in the process of completing her teaching credential and master's degree. I expressed to her that I would be opening a school soon, and that I would love to hire her when I had everything in place. A year later, I contacted her and asked if she was still interested in working at the school. Much to my surprise, she was! Not only did she accept my offer, she also jumped on board to support me in the process of pulling all of the loose ends together before the school opened. Teresa is still with the school today and she remains as committed to its success as she was 14 years ago.

Once I secured one teacher, the next hire came easily. I was telling someone I had just met about the school, and she mentioned her friend was teaching in the Los Angeles area but moving to Pasadena soon and looking for a job closer to home. I contacted the individual and she allowed me to observe her in her current classroom. At that time, she seem to fit the bill. Identifying and hiring my teachers was a huge relief, but I still had not secured a location, revenues to finance the project, nor students. None of this stopped my team. We kept the faith and continued to work toward opening the school. While looking for a site and seeking funding, we began recruiting students.

Roadblocks

Securing a location for the school site was another challenge that we faced. We found several locations and, one-by-one, each location fell through. It was frustrating; however, we learned that when one door closes, another one opens. I dug deep into my faith and began to understand that every step of this process would be a learning experience and preparation for God's ultimate plan.

I knew that God was in charge, and I needed to trust Him and the process. All the disappointments and setbacks tested my faith and presented learning experiences that were preparing me for my calling and divine purpose. Even before securing our location and funding, things were being put into motion as if the facility and funding were available. Recruiting students without a location was difficult. We distributed flyers to local preschools, and we held informational meetings at the local library and a community center. The initial group of parents who enrolled their children in kindergarten and 1st grade were pioneers. Though they didn't have much to go on, they were drawn to Rosebud Academy because of its mission and vision. They, too, wanted to be a part of something amazing.

A Miracle in the Making

In September of 2007, Pasadena Rosebud Academy Charter School opened its doors with 14 students, two teachers, an administrator, a business manager, and a few volunteers—pioneers in pursuit of educational excellence.

Starting off small would allow adjustments to be made with minimal disruption to the program. Although we knew what we wanted to do and what needed to happen, we realized that it was necessary to account for what we did not know. There were so many things to learn and many adjustments to make. The modifications were easy to make with a small staff, a small group of students, and a few parents. Beginning small meant opening with two classes: kindergarten and first grade. Miraculously, a few weeks before school started, we received a loan in the amount of $130,000. It wasn't much, but it allowed us to get started. In order to stay fiscally sound, my position, the administrator and the business manager did not take a salary for the first few years. Once the school opened, the majority of the income we received came from the state. It was based on the number of students enrolled and their average daily attendance. With just 14 students, the revenue generated from student attendance was minimal in the beginning, but by the grace of God, we made it work. It was amazing to witness the angels that He placed in our path to fill the financial gaps.

Today, we are still considered a small school. We currently serve roughly 200 students in grades K-8. We have a focus on linguistics, which addresses our goal to develop critical thinkers. In addition to critical thinking, our academy stands on core principles that include financial literacy, experience and exposure, global awareness, and service. Every year we take students on a variety of local field trips. Middle school students are afforded the opportunity to travel to Washington, D.C., New York, and Costa Rica. To date, we have taken two groups to China. Our holistic approach to educating students involves showing them how to be productive citizens and helping them understand that giving back is a part of their obligation as human beings. As we create a society, we have to educate and train our youth on how to continue the cycle of stewardship. Children have to learn their role in preserving the earth and contributing to humanity.

The Journey Continues

Pasadena Rosebud Academy continues to grow and evolve. Every year there are new experiences and a new set of obstacles to confront. As we tackle new challenges, it is an opportunity for me and my staff to grow exponentially. The mission and vision at Rosebud Academy continues to be at the forefront of our minds. As a team, we understand the ebb and flow of the work we do, though we continue to remain hopeful that our work will not be in vain. Our faith is strong, and we know that the work of our hearts will prevail in the end. The Rosebud team continues to be committed to changing the world, one child at a time.

Appendix B

The Purpose-Driven Educator's Oath

I, _____ ,
have been called to the profession of education, and I choose
to be obedient to that calling.

I pledge to:
- work toward the school's vision,
- maintain a high level of professionalism,
- use my creativity to perfect the art of education,
- hold **all** students to high social and academic standards,
- partner with parents for the greater good of the student,
- empathize with my students and parents,
- work with other educational leaders to enhance the educational experience for students, and
- do my part to dismantle systematic racism in education.

I take this oath as a commitment to myself, my students, my colleagues, and humanity.

Signature: _____

Date: _____

References

"1992 United States Men's Olympic Basketball Team." Wikipedia, accessed January 13, 2021. https://en.wikipedia.org/wiki/1992_United_States_men%27s_Olympic_basketball_team.

Bermúdez, Claudia and Hatkoff, Rebecca. "Orientation, Positionality, Classroom Ecology." Presentation at the Rosebud Academy Dismantling Racism Virtual Workshop, Pasadena, CA, February 2021.

Bressert, S. "What Is Emotional Intelligence (EQ)?" PsychCentral, last modified June 6, 2021. https://psychcentral.com/lib/what-is-emotional-intelligence-eq/.

"Business Culture: Introduction to Business Culture." Passport to Trade 2.0, accessed November 2020. https://businessculture.org/business-culture/.

"Equity in Education: What It Is and Why It Matters." Thinking Maps, published 2018; accessed November 2020.

Jacobson, Rae. "Metacognition: How Thinking About Thinking Can Help Kids." Child Mind Institute, accessed June 2020. https://childmind.org/article/how-metacognition-can-help-kids/.

Kaplan, Emily. "6 Essential Strategies for Teaching English Language Learners." Edutopia. George Lucas Educational Foundation, April 12, 2019. https://www.edutopia.org/article/6-essential-strategies-teaching-english-language-learners.

Lockley, Sina Kaye. "7 Reasons Why Internal Communication Is Important for Success." Staffbase, accessed March 2020 https://staffbase.com/blog/7-reasons-why-internal-communication-is-important-for-success/.

Marriner, David Merill, Charles Reigeluth, Robert Mills Gagné,

Jerome Bruner, and Roger Schank. "Cognitivism." Learning Theories, accessed December 2020. https://www.learning-theories.com/cognitivism.html.

Mastin, L. "Existence and Consciousness." The Basics of Philosophy. January 2009. https://www.philosophybasics.com/branch_metaphysics.html.

McLeod, Dr. Saul. "Maslow's Hierarchy of Needs." Simply Psychology, last updated December 29, 2020. https://www.simplypsychology.org/maslow.html.

Partners in Leadership. "4 Steps to Develop Your AQ and Make Change Happen." Inc. July 26, 2016. https://www.inc.com/partners-in-leadership/4-steps-to-develop-your-aq-and-make-change-happen.html.

Saaris, Dr. Natalie. "Mastering Metacognition: The What Why, and How." Actively Learn. February 23, 2017. https://www.activelylearn.com/post/metacognition.

Solar, Aria. "Best Practices for Your Internal Communication Strategy." Sprout Social. March 26, 2021. https://sproutsocial.com/insights/internal-communications-guide/.

Watson, John B., Ivan Pavlov, B. F. Skinner, E. L. Thorndike, and Albert Bandura. "Behaviorism." Learning Theories, accessed December 2019. https://www.learning-theories.com/behaviorism.html.

What is an Individualized Educational Plan?. Access Computing The Alliance for Access to Computing Careers. 2006-2021 University of Washington (UW). accessed September 19, 2021. https://www.washington.edu/accesscomputing/what-individualized-education-plan

"What is the AQ? The Adaptability Quotient for Beginners." ForbesBooks, accessed July 2020. https://forbesbooks.com/adaptability-quotient/.

Key Terms

Achievement gap: The disparity in academic achievement between African American, Hispanic, and Native American students and their Asian and White counterparts.

Classroom ecology: All interactions between teachers, students, curriculum, and the classroom environment that contribute to students' learning experiences. Classroom ecology can be productive or toxic. Teachers can use their presence and classroom culture, climate, physical layout, routines, norms, expectations, language etc. to cultivate a productive, anti-racist classroom ecology that limits the need for discipline policies.

Crescendo: The X-factor, or unexplainable quality, of a teacher. It is instinctive and innate, transcending knowledge and practice, and it can't be taught at the university. The crescendo represents the soul of a teacher and how they show up in their educational practice. Educators have a Crescendo Aptitude (CA) on a scale ranging from 0-10.

EduHarmony: The practice of connecting the right employees with the right employer in the educational system.

Equitable Educational Success: The process by which parents, students, educators, politicians, and society at-large work collectively toward the academic success of African American, Hispanic, and Native American students, thus closing the achievement gap.

Fundamental interview questions: Generic questions that an employer asks all potential employees. These secondary questions help to establish how well the candidate will perform at their position.

Individual Educational Program/Plan (IEP): This is a plan or program developed to ensure that a child with an identified disability who is attending an elementary or secondary educational institution receives specialized instruction and related services. The IEP is developed by a team of individuals from various educational disciplines, the child with a disability, family members, and/or designated advocates.

Individual Employee Personality (IEP): The specific traits or characteristics that show up in the work environment that define the employee both personally and professionally. The IEP defines not only who they are, but what matters to them.

Leadership Congruency Postulate: The idea or understanding that every staff member, regardless of their title, is a leader. The postulate further suggests that the hierarchy of leadership at any given time can be at any level. Each position holds the highest ranking of power at certain times during the day, week, month, and year.

Leading interview questions: Questions created based on the information found or not found in the application, résumé, and letters of recommendation. These questions are specific questions related to the candidates.

Vitality: The capacity for survival or for the continuation of a meaningful or purposeful existence. It can be further described as the power to live, grow, or develop. In education, vitality is how schools will grow and thrive to create long-term success for all students, which will, in turn, contribute to the flourishing of society and humanity.

Warm demanders: Teachers who hold students to high standards. They convince students that they have great minds and earn their trust to get them to learn.

Acknowledgments

There have been many individuals who have played a meaningful role in my life as I've grown both personally and professionally. I am extremely grateful to all who have impacted me and my life's work. I would be remiss if I didn't acknowledge those who have directly and indirectly contributed to and supported the publishing of *The Purpose-Driven School*. To start, I would like to thank my son JoJo, for his input and guidance on the thoughts and ideas that have helped to shape this book. To my daughter Sydney, I want to thank her for her continuous inspiration. She is and has always been a voice of encouragement.

The ideas found in this book are based on my personal educational journey from preschool to college and more than 25 years of working in the field of education. The principles and practices detailed in this book are informed by my experiences and the guidance and wisdom I received from master thinkers around the world. Over the years, I have read many books and listened to countless speakers who provided me with inspiration, direction, and wisdom on my personal and professional development. Their words of wisdom have helped me on my own purpose-driven journey as an educator and further equipped me with the knowledge and insight to write this book. They confirmed what I have learned from my practice and gave me the motivation, confidence, and determination to share my knowledge. Ultimately, God has been my primary source of guidance, strength, and motivation. All of the words, ideas, and concepts come from His influence on my life.

I would also like to acknowledge and express sincere gratitude for my Master Mind Group of peer readers, editors, and critics: Tiffany Bell, Joseph Brumfield II, Kathy Castleberry, Pamela Dansby, and Arlani Harris. Your comments and feedback have been extremely valuable and important to the production of this book.

Last but not least, a special thanks goes to Prentice Deadrick, the former PUSD board member who fought for Pasadena Rosebud Academy and was a steadfast supporter when the odds were against us. Scott Phelps was another proponent for the approval of Rosebud Academy, and to him I am also grateful. Without the enthusiasm of these two individuals, Pasadena Rosebud Academy would not exist—and this book would not be possible.

About the Author

SHAWN BROWN-BRUMFIELD is the founder and executive director of Pasadena Rosebud Academy Charter School. She was called to the field of education after receiving her bachelor's degree in economics. Ms. Brown has been an educational practitioner for over 25 years and continues to serve as an educational leader, advocate, and mentor. She is a proud mom of two amazing children. She currently resides in California with her children.